USING INDUSTRY ANALYSIS FOR STRATEGIC INTELLIGENCE

Capabilities and Strategic Intent

by Chuck Howe

National Intelligence University
Washington, DC

January 2015

 *Using Industry Analysis for Strategic Intelligence: Capabilities and Strategic Intent*

In Chuck Howe's *Using Industry Analysis for Strategic Intelligence: Capabilities and Strategic Intent*, the author argues that the Intelligence Community should evaluate globalization as a strategic factor affecting interdependencies between nations. He outlines a variety of industry analysis techniques—including the Five Forces Model, the External Environment Model, and the Value Chain Model—that could be valuable to analysts. Using the semiconductor industry as a case study, Howe illustrates methods that analysts should use in deriving strategic insights from industrial capability.

Using Industry Analysis for Strategic Intelligence is part of the National Intelligence (NI) Press Occasional Paper Series. Occasional Papers examine topics of unique value to the Intelligence Community.

The goal of the NI Press is to publish high-quality, valuable, and timely books on topics of concern to the Intelligence Community and the U.S. government. Books published by the NI Press undergo peer review by senior officials in the U.S. government and by outside experts.

This publication has been cleared for unrestricted distribution. The views expressed in this publication are those of the author and do not necessarily reflect the official policy or position of the Department of Defense, the Intelligence Community, or the U.S. government. Authors of NI Press publications enjoy full academic freedom, provided that they do not disclose classified information, jeopardize operations security, or misrepresent official U.S. policy. Such academic freedom empowers authors to offer new and sometimes controversial perspectives in the interest of furthering debate on key issues.

ACKNOWLEDGMENTS

First and foremost, I thank Jeff Stillman, in the Office of Analytic Integrity and Standards, for leaving my fellowship research proposal on the "stack" for consideration by the ODNI Exceptional Analyst Fellowship selection committee. Even though I am not an intelligence analyst, he recognized the value of a different perspective, and throughout encouraged my project.

Also critical to the existence of this project was the support of my leadership in AT&F, especially Wally Coggins, to gap my position for the year and allow me the time to research, write, and produce this introduction to industry analysis for the analytic community.

Many thanks to current and former faculty members at the Industrial College of the Armed Forces (now Dwight D. Eisenhower School for National Security and Resource Strategy). There are several war colleges in the Department of Defense, but only one Industrial College. Drs. Linda Brandt and Rich Shipe reviewed my research proposal and spent even more of their time to provide an outside review of the manuscript. When I was a student at ICAF many years ago, Dr. Gerald Abbott introduced me to the primary sources on industry structure economics and analysis; I appreciate his continuing mentorship in this subject area. Last, but not least, CAPT Susan Maybaumwisniewski, USN (ret.), a former colleague at ICAF, now at BENS, provided early brainstorming and outline direction to this project—a wonderful person to kick an idea around with.

I would be remiss if I did not mention the semiconductor industry that I have followed for the last six years. There are no better representatives than the outstanding people at SEMI and EDAC. They are exemplars of an industry that is always willing to educate others on the challenges they face at the leading edge of this global industry.

I started my understanding of the analytic community by taking Analysis 101 and Open Source Academy courses. It was great meeting the "up-and-coming" crop of intelligence analysts, and they showed me they had the wherewithal to try new analytic methods. Outside of the classroom, the development of the industry analysis methodology was aided immeasurably by the meetings with analysts across the Intelligence Community. At each of meetings I would repeat the mantra "industry analysis models are a tool, not a solution," to assure the analyst I was looking to complement their analytical skill set. Intelligence analysts remain the target audience for this book, and it is hoped that they will add it to their toolkit.

In my travels across the analytic community, I came upon a small but very productive team at the Institute for Analysis. They listened to and critiqued several iterations of my project, and their director, Donn Treese, even provided an outside review of the manuscript.

Dr. Cathryn Thurston, the acting vice president of OOR, provided unflagging support to this book, even when that support had to compete with construction projects, the relocation of the office, staff departures to early retirements, and the never-ending lineup of master's thesis aspirants at NDIC (now NIU). Her editorial direction on draft submissions kept my initial intent intact, while greatly improving its delivery.

Finally, I want to recognize my wife, Cindy, an extraordinary teacher, for her unfailing support throughout this endeavor. Thank you, Cindy.

Contents

Chapter One: Introduction 1
    Organization of Discussion 3
    Background 3
    Globalization and National Competitiveness 3
    Role of Intelligence Community: 1950s to 1980s 4
    Moving Intelligence Community Out of Its Comfort Zone 6
    Competing Analysis: Short-Term Crises and Long-Term Problems 7

Chapter Two: Industry Analysis 9
    Overview of Financial Activity of Firm 10
    Porter Five Forces Model 11
    External Environment Model 14
    Value Chain Model 16

Chapter Three: Putting It All Together—The Five Steps 21
    Step 1: Select the Industry 21
    Step 2: Define the Industry 23
    Step 3: Identify Sources of Information 27
    Step 4: Collect Information 29
        Industry Observations from Data Collection 32
    Step 5: Analyze Results 52
        East Asia: Semiconductor Industry 52
        Strategic Intelligence Insight 58

Chapter Four: Conclusion 69
    Conclusion 69

Contents continued

Applying Industry Analysis 69

Follow the Steps 69

Utility of Industry Analysis 70

Increased Attention by the Intelligence Community to
Globalization 71

APPENDIXES

Appendix A: External Environment Model Segments
and Elements 73

Appendix B: Semiconductor Industry Tutorial 75

Appendix C: Information Sources Specific to
Semiconductor Industry 89

BIBLIOGRAPHY 95

ABOUT THE AUTHOR 123

USING INDUSTRY ANALYSIS FOR STRATEGIC INTELLIGENCE

Chapter One

Introduction

The U.S. Intelligence Community needs to augment its primary focus on political and military dimensions to address the potential for strategic surprise due to the changing nature of business, industry, and national competitiveness in a global economy. The Council on Competitiveness, a nonpartisan, nongovernmental organization of American chief executive officers, university presidents, and labor leaders, highlights the complex nature of these changes (see box).[1]

Lens of Competitiveness

A rising standard of living for all Americans is not guaranteed. The United States now operates in a truly global economy:

- Companies are outsourcing and spreading their value chains globally

- Hundreds of nations are trading tens of trillions of dollars daily in the financial markets

- Strong markets and talent pools have emerged in the developing world

- Businesses and governments operate across highly integrated regional economies

- Vast communications networks allow for immediate global connectivity and information transfer and also create unprecedented vulnerabilities

- New risks, such as competition for natural resources, climate change and terrorism, now affect the competitiveness of countries, companies, and communities

Whether our citizens and businesses will thrive in the new global economy depends largely on our ability to understand and act upon these prevailing forces of change and attract high-value economic activity to regions across America.

Source: Council on Competitiveness, *www.compete.org*.

The opening observations from the Council on Competitiveness highlight the major strategic shifts in a *global* economy and their importance to our country. The developing economies of the world are driving these shifts, and their industrial capability is a major component of their success. Analyzing an industry in another country or region of the world can yield strategic insights about a nation's capabilities and strategic intent.

While the U.S. Intelligence Community is aware of the discussion, as evidenced in the 2009 *National Intelligence Strategy*, it still needs to pay closer attention to the strategic implications of these changes. In particular, intelligence analysts must be able to gauge the global competitiveness of other nations in order to ensure that this dimension is a consideration in strategic assessments.

A key indicator of competitiveness is industrial capability. A nation's industrial capability is an economic engine, producing jobs, growth, and ultimately prosperity. Developed and developing nations realize this and want to build an industrial engine to reap the benefits. Relatively recent advances in information technology that produce unprecedented amounts of open-source information help these nations.[2] Business strategists and competitive intelligence professionals use many analysis tools to mine the plethora of open sources—to understand the plans and intentions of other firms and the global market—so that they can achieve a competitive advantage.

Although the Intelligence Community is not collecting information on individual businesses, it is interested in national- or regional-level plans and aspirations. To shed light on sometimes-opaque economic plans and strategic intentions, the all-source intelligence analyst can use open-source data, industry analysis tools, and a nation's interest in growing its economy.

In short, a nation's policy and investment decisions to grow and sustain its industrial capability are visible through their interactions with industry. The thesis of this book is that an all-source intelligence analyst can employ the analysis tools of business strategists and competitive intelligence professionals to develop strategic intelligence insights regarding a nation's plans and intentions.

USING INDUSTRY ANALYSIS FOR STRATEGIC INTELLIGENCE

Organization of Discussion

To support the thesis and intelligence focus of this book, the remaining chapters of this book are all oriented toward the all-source analyst. The book consists of four chapters. This first chapter provides general background information, to help orient the reader. Chapter 2 introduces industry analysis and proposes a methodology for application in the Intelligence Community. Chapter 3 describes the five steps an all-source analyst would go through to provide inputs for an intelligence assessment. Chapter 4 presents concluding discussions on the value of industry analysis to the U.S. Intelligence Community. There are also three appendixes. Appendix A provides a template for one of the industry analysis models presented in Chapter 2. Appendixes B and C, respectively, provide a semiconductor tutorial, as well as information related to the semiconductor industry—of use in understanding the discussion in the main chapters.

Background

Before starting our discussion of industry analysis and its application, there are two personal observations operating in the background.[3] The first is that globalization and its potential for strategic impact on national competitiveness has not yet grabbed the full attention of the Intelligence Community. The second observation concerns the Intelligence Community's grasp of other nations' industrial capabilities; outside of leading-edge science and technology, defense issues, dual-use technologies, and nonproliferation, the Intelligence Community is largely silent. The following two subsections briefly provide the background for these observations.

Globalization and National Competitiveness

The term *globalization* has many definitions. Suzanne Berger, in her book *How We Compete: What Companies around the World Are Doing to Make It in Today's Global Economy*, describes globalization as "the acceleration of the processes in the international economy and in domestic economies that operate toward unifying world markets."[4] These changes and the domestic concerns they cause are not unprecedented. There was an earlier period bracketing the turn of the nineteenth century that also saw the same levels of capital mobility, trade, and immigration among countries. This early period of globalization was broken by World War I, and it was not until the 1980s that the world economy returned to the same high levels of capital mobility, foreign direct investment, and trade. An important point regarding the end of this earlier period of globalization is that nations were largely able to shut off their ties to the outside world (from the 1920s through the 1980s) and continue economic growth.

Role of the Intelligence Community: 1950s to 1980s

A look at the history of the Intelligence Community, specifically foreign economic intelligence during the Cold War, reveals that one of the stated purposes, "To assist in divining the intentions of potential enemies in the conviction that how they act in the economic sphere is likely to reveal intentions," generated a lot of support for industry-sector analysis.[5]

This initial interest in industry-sector analysis in the early years of the Cold War was also due to a sense among policymakers that the Soviet Union could possibly outperform the United States economically and militarily.[6] To address this concern, the Central Intelligence Agency devoted considerable analytical resources to industry studies. These studies of selected sectors are characterized as assessing

> the strengths, weaknesses, and prospects of these sectors in detail and on a continuing basis. These studies generally had a special focus on the technological level of the given industry. They supported not only intelligence objectives but, as contributions to publications of the Joint Economic Committee of Congress, contributed to the general pool of knowledge on the Soviet economy.[7]

These analyses focused on vulnerabilities in the Soviet economy and, especially, areas where progress could hamper their economic development. As the Cold War progressed, increasing emphasis on international and military topics resulted in the transfer of analyst resources away from Soviet economic performance and specific industry-sector analysis of the Soviet Union.[8]

USING INDUSTRY ANALYSIS FOR STRATEGIC INTELLIGENCE

While it is clear that globalization and the practice of industry analysis by the Intelligence Community are not unprecedented, what has been the role of the Intelligence Community in more recent experience? Michael L. Dertouzos, Richard K. Lester, and Robert M. Solow, a group of MIT researchers, made this prediction in their 1989 book, *Made in America*:

> To live well, a nation must produce well. In recent years many observers have charged that American industry is not producing as well as it ought to produce, or as well as it used to produce, or as well as the industries of some other nations have learned to produce. If the charges are true and if the trend cannot be reversed, then sooner or later, the American standard of living must pay the penalty.[9]

Mark Lowenthal describes the corresponding debate in the Intelligence Community at that time:

> During the late 1980s some people maintained that several of these issues (overseas competitiveness, trading relations, foreign economic espionage, **industrial espionage** undertaken by businesses, and possible countermeasures) could be addressed, in part, through a closer connection between intelligence and U.S. businesses [emphasis in original]. Few advocates of closer intelligence–business collaboration, however, had substantial answers for some of the more compelling questions that it raised (which is one reason that this approach was quickly rejected).[10]

This description is the most up-to-date open-source assessment of the Intelligence Community's consideration of industry analysis. In 2006, Suzanne Berger, who was a major contributor to the work of Dertouzos et al., the MIT group that provided important observations and prescriptions in *Made in America*, released the book *How We Compete*. In it, Berger observed that all of the industry prescriptions they had made in 1989 had become the basic operating code of American companies. But Berger also said, "[A]mong our greatest concerns today is one that was not on the list in the 1980s—how to make good companies and good jobs stick in the United States."[11] She further observed:

> Then, our challenge seemed to be import penetration. Today, the fragmentation of the system of production has changed the problem. Now it's the prospect that the resources available to companies abroad—and well-educated and lower cost workers are one of the main attractions—will induce businesses to shift their activities abroad.

Globalization is upon us, and, unlike the early twentieth century, nations cannot "turn it off" and build or sustain industrial capability.

Moving the Intelligence Community Out of Its Comfort Zone

The Intelligence Community's internal discussions in the 1980s about sharing intelligence with business to foster our national competitiveness should not be confused with what is being advocated here—the development of strategic intelligence insights from understanding the development of industrial capability *in other nations* and the consideration of these strategic insights in producing intelligence products for our national policymakers. Although globalization is all around us, the *National Intelligence Strategy* fails to push the Intelligence Community out of the traditional political-military sphere.[12] As Fareed Zakaria observes of America's traditional perspective, "At the political-military level, we remain in a single-superpower world. But in every other dimension—industrial, financial, educational, social, cultural—the distribution of power is shifting, moving away from American dominance."[13]

To be fair, the Intelligence Community is not ignoring globalization; it is just not actively pursuing it. But a closer look at the first of its four strategic goals in the 2009 *National Intelligence Strategy*, "Enable wise national security policies," could provide an avenue for collection and analysis of trends in globalization.[14] In support of that goal, the Intelligence Community further explains it "will provide policymakers with strategic intelligence that helps them understand countries, regions, issues, and the potential outcomes of their decisions. We will also provide feedback to policymakers on the impact of their decisions."[15] So, if the Intelligence Community is aware of globalization and one of its strategic goals could support analysis of global trends, what is the argument for operating outside its spheres of comfort by taking a closer look at other nations' industrial capability?

USING INDUSTRY ANALYSIS FOR STRATEGIC INTELLIGENCE

Competing Analysis: Short-Term Crises and Long-Term Problems

We cannot ignore that the Intelligence Community is heavily engaged in our nation's current overseas military commitments. Plus, the Intelligence Community is also charged with addressing transnational issues, such as criminal organizations, failed states, ungoverned spaces, the global economic crisis, climate change, energy competition, rapid technological change, and dissemination of information.[16] But the main question of this book is: who in the Intelligence Community is monitoring the industrial capabilities of other nations and regions, which may have a major impact on American interests and security?

While the National Intelligence Council provides a forecast of economic changes occurring over the next 15 years, these observations are based on general trends forecasting major economic shifts, strategic materials, and energy.[17] Outside of the Intelligence Community, there is already recognition of the need for new tools to understand and communicate the nature of global economic integration. Timothy Sturgeon highlights that "studies that rely solely on macro-level statistics such as trade and investment cannot help but render invisible the detailed contours of the world economy."[18] The main point here is that while statistics and analysis on global economic information are readily available for purchase over the Internet, there is also strategic intelligence of interest to the Intelligence Community and policymakers in the "contours." The tools and methods used by industry analysts highlighted in the following chapters will enable the all-source analyst to see some of the contours in the world economy and gain strategic intelligence insights of use to national policymakers.

The opening observations from the Council on Competitiveness highlight the major strategic shifts in a *global* economy and their importance to our country. The developing economies of the world are driving these shifts, and their industrial capability is a major component of their success. Analyzing an industry in another country or region of the world can yield strategic insights about a nation's capabilities and strategic intent. Chapter 2 introduces industry analysis and proposes a methodology for applying it in the Intelligence Community.

Chapter Two

Industry Analysis

There are innumerable analytical tools employed in business. Our purpose is to identify and employ the analytical tools that can provide strategic insights into a nation's industrial capability. The industry analysis involves a detailed review of the external and competitive forces that influence the way an industry develops.[19] This is what sets industry analysis apart from an all-source analyst simply performing a keyword search for information sources about an industry. The three analytical tools discussed here are widely used in business. They are the Porter Five Forces Model, the External Environment Model, and the Value Chain Model.

Long-term background preparation for this book—and in particular selection of these three analytical models—stems from various sources: experience as an acquisition officer in the Department of Defense; early exposure to the disciplines of business and industry analysis as part of preparing for a master's of business administration degree; continuing professional education at the Industrial College of the Armed Forces (ICAF), analyzing industry sectors and their importance to national security, as well as learning to look beyond the numbers to appreciate the strategic interplay between government and industry; and teaching industry analysis to graduate-level students at ICAF, where use of the Five Forces Model and the Value Chain Model proved the most valuable for students to appreciate the structure of an industry, and where use of the External Environment Model broadened their understanding of the interaction between industry and government. The open-source methodology and data-collection approaches for this book resulted from that experience at ICAF.

That said, the industry analysis approach introduced in this chapter and elaborated on in the following chapters is easily understood and does not require the intelligence analyst to have a business or technical background. In fact, the intelligence analyst may have a head start in comprehending its application due to his or her training in other analysis techniques, such as the analysis of competing hypotheses. To begin our discussion of the industry analysis models, we will start with a brief look at the nature of a firm or corporation.

Overview of the Financial Activity of a Firm

A firm's performance has two components—survival and profitability.[20] The measure of survival is obvious, but the profitability component is measured by profit maximization, whereby a firm determines the price and quantity of output that delivers the greatest profit. Figure 2.1 provides a top-level view of a firm's financial activity.

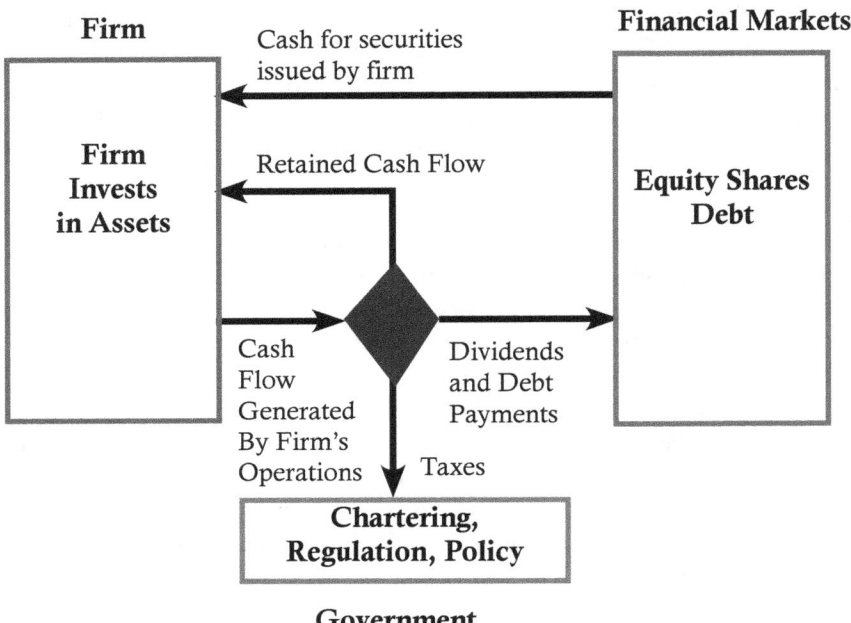

Figure 2.1: Financial Activity of a Firm[21]

Figure 2.1 shows that the firm (red block) generates cash by issuing stocks to or borrowing from financial markets (blue block). The firm uses this cash in developing goods or services and the resulting cash flow generated is then used within the firm (retained earnings), paid out to the financial community (stock dividends, debt repayments), and paid to the government (taxes).

This simple model allows the reader to visualize the effects of a country's public policy, financial, or market announcements that are reported regarding a firm or even an entire industry. For example, when a government announces a 10-year exemption for the collection of any taxes from a firm that relocates to their country, the firm can now use more of its cash flow, via retained earnings, to fund research and development, buy additional assets, or use it to enhance its standing with the financial community by retiring debt or increasing dividends. The reality is much more complex, but this basic model and the economic maxim of profit maximization are useful for understanding interactions between governments and industry.

Academics studying business and industry economics develop models by observing how firms organize and perform against their competitors and in the marketplace. As the business world changes, these academic communities find some insights to be timeless, while others are modified or even discarded. Businesses also use many of these models to analyze their competitors. The Strategic and Competitive Intelligence Professionals (SCIP) organization bridges the academic and business world and provides good sources for exploring and discussing the methods of competitive intelligence.[22] According to Robert Grant's *Contemporary Strategy Analysis*, one of the most comprehensive industry texts, competitive intelligence has three main purposes:

- Forecast competitors' future strategies and decisions.

- Predict competitors' likely reactions to a firm's strategic initiatives.

- Determine how competitors' behavior can be influenced to make it more favorable.[23]

In academia and the competitive world of business, as long as the models and associated analytical methods are of use, they will survive—although not without some tailoring. The following discussion will describe the key elements of each model. This will help the all-source analyst to understand the industry structure to the extent that it yields, in combination with the other models, strategic intelligence insights regarding a nation's plans and intentions.

Porter Five Forces Model

The first model carries the name of its developer, Michael Porter of Harvard University. Porter arguably produced the seminal text on industry analysis, *Competitive Strategy*, which describes his Five Forces Model.[24] The model is meant to convey the forces acting on an industry. Our usage of the model is very different from that of the business analyst who is working to understand competitors. For our collection purposes, the Five Forces Model provides a mental construct to use in reviewing and determining which data to keep for further analysis. For example, when reading an article, is it possible to determine who is the buyer and who is the supplier? What is the threat of product substitution if prices rise too high? What are the barriers to entry to the industry? Can a government overcome this barrier to entry through policy decisions? How intense is competition within the industry? Is the intensity of competition inviting government involvement? Today, thirty years later, the business community still uses this model to describe their industry and gain insights into how it is changing.

In economic terms, an industry can be defined as "a group of firms producing products that are close substitutes."[25] The Five Forces Model, shown in Figure 2.2, is meant to convey the primary forces that affect the structure and conduct of the industry. In business, the end result of conducting industry analysis via the Five Forces Model is a description of the industry that the company will use to determine a strategy it will pursue in the future. The main point is that a firm does not want to pursue a strategy that is not going to lead to a competitive advantage. For the intelligence analyst, however, the end result of conducting industry analysis via the Five Forces Model is a conceptual understanding of the industry that will then aid in the collection and analysis of information on the industry in all of its global locations.

Figure 2.2 shows the five forces affecting the structure and conduct of an industry: threat of new entrants, bargaining power of buyers, bargaining power of suppliers, threat of substitute products or services, and rivalry among existing competitors.

The *threat of new entrants* concerns how easily a new competitor emerges from outside the industry. Intense price competition is one sign that it is easy for other firms to enter into the industry. And if it is easy for new entrants to appear, firms already in the industry may choose to pursue future investment opportunities outside of the industry. Examples of barriers to entry are large capital costs for plants and equipment, unique process or product technologies, and government regulation.

USING INDUSTRY ANALYSIS FOR STRATEGIC INTELLIGENCE

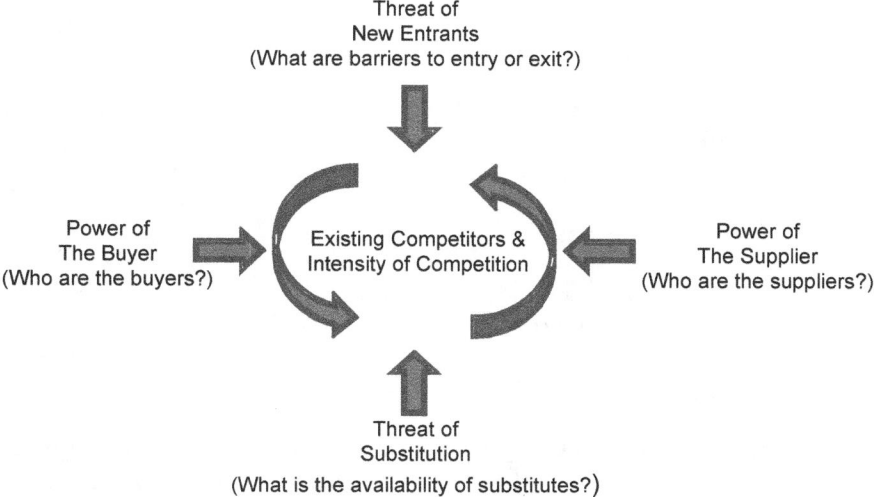

Figure 2.2: Porter Five Forces Model[26]

The *bargaining power of the buyer or supplier* is meant to capture the extent to which the industry determines the prices in their industry. If suppliers to the industry hold a unique material required for an industry to continue, then they may temporarily hold an advantage in setting prices for the industry. Similarly, if the buyers of the industry product or service have a lot of power, they can dictate prices or demand features in the products they buy. The word "temporary" applies in all of these cases, as industry and business operate in dynamic environments.

The *threat of substitution* concerns the potential for buyers to buy substitute products or services if the industry demands high prices or does not respond to buyer requirements.

The *rivalry among competitors* is central to the Five Forces Model. This is the intensity of competition among firms and the characteristics of that competition. One obvious factor in the intensity of the rivalry is market growth (slowing, increasing); a not-so-obvious factor is exit costs. A company in an industry with intense rivalries may find few options for pursuing other ventures (including exiting) due to large investments in plants and equipment (e.g., automotive industry, oil refining industry). Contrast this last point with the earlier discussion on the threat of new entrants.

In summary, the Five Forces Model captures the key factors that determine the profits earned by firms in an industry, the value of the product to the buyer, the power of the supplier to set prices, and the intensity of competition.

External Environment Model

For the business analyst, the External Environment Model complements the Five Forces Model in support of business planning. But for our purposes, we will use the External Environment Model as our collection framework to gain strategic insights into a nation's capabilities and strategic intent.

The External Environment Model moves our inward-looking frame of reference for the industry outward to the strategic level.[27] The premise behind considering the external environment is simply that firms and industries operate in an environment that can have a large impact on their competitiveness. While the external environment has an effect on the structure and conduct of an industry and the firms within, the specific segments of the external environment for examination will vary according to the user. These different segments are often denoted by the acronyms applied to the External Environment Model in use. For example, "PEST" stands for political/legal, economic, social, and technological segments, while "STEEP" refers to social, technological, economic, ecological, and political/legal segments.[28] Reflecting the increasing emphasis on "green" issues, there is also "STEER," which stands for socio-cultural, technological, economic, ecological, and regulatory segments.[29] The definition of the segments selected is all oriented toward identifying external forces or impacts on the industry. For example, referring to PEST, one aspect of the political/legal segment is looking for the degree to which government regulation directs or influences the conduct of industry. One element of the economic segment is the impact of the global economy on the domestic economy and markets. Another element of the social segment is workforce education and skill levels, and an element of the technological segment is the level and focus of government expenditures for research and development.

USING INDUSTRY ANALYSIS FOR STRATEGIC INTELLIGENCE

While the selection and definition of segments vary, the important point for our purposes is the value of having a framework to guide the collection of information for further analysis. And these models can be combined to make new models, too. For example, Fleisher developed the Nine Forces Model by applying STEEP/PEST factors in conjunction with the Five Forces Model (four PEST segments plus five forces equals nine forces).[30] Similarly, we will also integrate the knowledge we gain from the Porter Five Forces Model with relevant external segments to form a generic overview of an industry from both inside and out. Figure 2.3 shows a framework displaying the segments and elements we will use to collect information (a step discussed later).

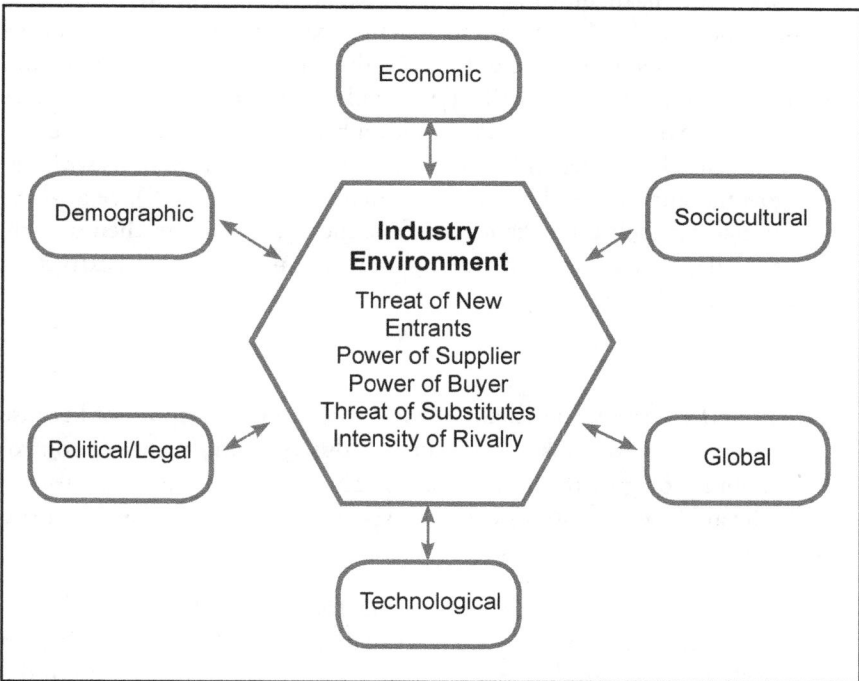

Figure 2.3: Framework for Information Collection[31]

The hexagon in the middle of the figure represents the industry environment and lists the forces described by the Five Forces Model. The segments arrayed around the hexagon represent the external environment that surrounds an industry. The segments of this framework are not cast in stone, and one does not have to collect information on every element. Appendix A lists the segments and their constituent elements for this framework. When reading about an industry, the analyst should use the segments and elements, and include the five forces, as a template for categorizing, sorting, and saving information. This approach is subjective, but useful, because all of the data will be collated and have source documentation.

In summary, the External Environment Model, which encompasses the Five Forces Model, captures the key external factors that influence the profits earned by firms in an industry and the intensity of competition. For our purposes, analysts should be able to use the External Environment Model to form a mental picture of the industry as they perform data collection and analysis. It is important to clarify that, while in business, the Five Forces and External Environment Models provide a basis for strategic planning, we are focusing on identifying and understanding industry interactions with national governments to develop strategic intelligence insights. Once analysts have internalized their understanding of the industry, they can then quickly perform the day-to-day task of reviewing industry information and extracting any strategic intelligence insights.

Value Chain Model

The final model is the Value Chain Model. This model is important because it identifies the fundamental activities in an industry that influence or control the profitability or growth of an industry. These key activities are also frequently the areas where nations exercise export controls for national-security or national-competitiveness reasons.

The Value Chain Model provides a contextual framework for review and evaluation of information. Are there activities that are not only key (hence are on the value chain), but also determine or control growth or profitability in the industry? For example, a country concerned about national competitiveness may focus its attention on those key activities that determine the growth of that industry.

The Value Chain Model was introduced to the broader business community in the 1980s.[32] The value chain, as originally envisioned, is oriented toward

USING INDUSTRY ANALYSIS FOR STRATEGIC INTELLIGENCE

the firm and, in large corporations, the business unit. The example provided in Figure 2.4 is a visualization of the value chain discussed in Porter's book, *The Competitive Advantage of Nations.*

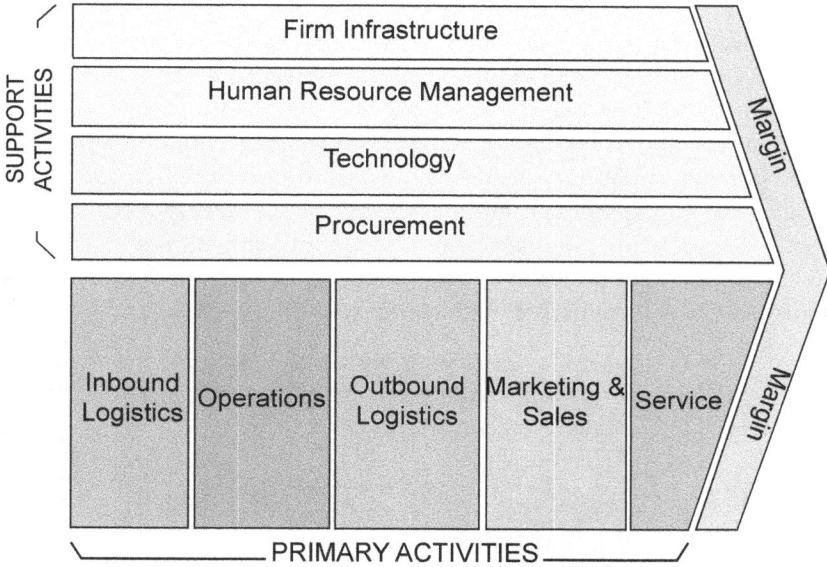

Figure 2.4: Value Chain (© Dinesh Pratap Singh)[33]

A firm using the Value Chain Model will lay out its major activities and then systematically evaluate how each activity adds value to the firm. Business analysts understand that this analysis also includes the relative performance of competitors in executing those activities. This approach supports the firm's strategic planning to achieve competitive advantage.

For Porter's purposes 30 years ago, applying the value chain to anything above the level of the firm (to the industry or sector level) would not shed much light on the unique value that the firm had in creating competitive advantage. Back then, the value chains of U.S. industry were primarily domestic. Multinational firms had overseas subsidiaries in place to deliver products from domestic U.S. value chains. Today, however, multinational corporations base many parts of the value chain, including product development and manufacturing processes, in many regions and countries. Lifting the value chain to the industry level begins to make sense.

For our purposes, we will exclusively focus on developing the value chain at the industry level. The Intelligence Community is not interested in the competitive advantage of individual firms; our focus is on understanding the structure and conduct of an industry and the strategic intelligence insights its interactions with other nations can provide. Fortunately, there is a body of work in academe that applies the Value Chain Model in describing the scope and scale of globalization, including how industries organize to operate in a global environment.[34] For example, Timothy Sturgeon's work recognizes that development of many products is now the result of global value chains. Academicians seeking to understand the governance of such far-flung industries identify several different types of global value chain governance (Figure 2.5).

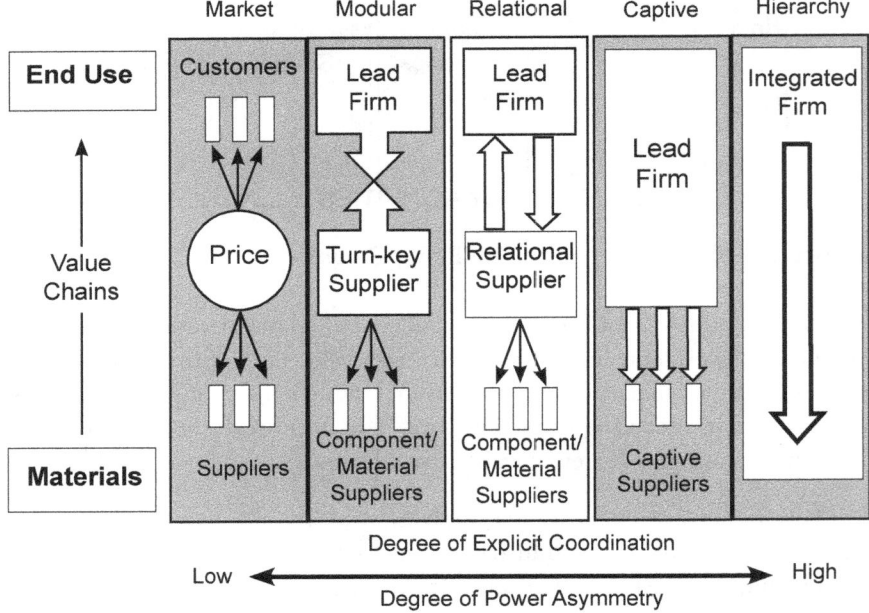

Figure 2.5: Global Value Chain Governance (© Taylor & Francis Group)[35]

USING INDUSTRY ANALYSIS FOR STRATEGIC INTELLIGENCE

Figure 2.5 shows both vertical and horizontal integration by governance type. At the far left, the value chains flow "up" from materials to end use. Arranged horizontally across the bottom is the degree of coordination required between activities and the degree of power asymmetry. Within the value chain examples, the black arrows indicate where price is the only interaction between activities in the value chain, and the solid white arrows indicate where information is included in the interaction. Looking at the far right, the integrated firm maintains competency in all facets of that industries' value chain. At the far left, the most basic value chain, the market, is a price-based market with multiple suppliers and customers communicating only via price. The models in-between show varying complex, symbiotic relationships between suppliers and buyers within the value chain. As one moves from basic to more complex value chains, the development of standards and the ability to exchange information far more complex than pricing information are major facilitators for the development of a global value chain. For now, these global value chain governance models should be kept in the background; they will be of more use when we select and analyze an industry.

In summary, the Value Chain Model captures the key value-added activities of the industry, and the Governance Model shows the level of complexity of the value chain. Developing or being able to interpret the value chain for the industry under analysis is an important early step in understanding the industry. Internalizing an understanding of the industry value chain also contributes to the day-to-day task of reviewing industry information and extracting any strategic intelligence insights.

The firm is the fundamental business unit, and a group of firms that produce similar products are collectively referred to as an industry. This chapter has so far provided three basic models to help the analyst frame the scope of industry analysis. The Porter Five Forces Model helps in understanding the forces influencing the conduct and structure of industry via the power of the buyer and supplier to set prices, the threat of substitution and new entrants to the industry, and the intensity of the existing competition. For our purposes, the analyst can use the Five Forces Model to form a mental picture of the industry. The External Environment Model identifies how and to what extent firms and the industries in which they reside interact with the external environment. For our purposes, the analyst will use the External Environment Model segments and elements in developing the collection plan (discussed later). The Value Chain Model will become central to the analyst's understanding of the industry under analysis, and also provides a context for reviewing information regarding the industry.

Chapter Three

Putting It All Together—The Five Steps

This chapter discusses how the all-source analyst, covering a region or country desk, includes commercial industry when tasked to provide inputs for an intelligence assessment. There are five steps in the process used by the analyst: (1) select an industry, (2) define the industry, (3) identify sources of information, (4) collect information, and (5) analyze results. The five steps are described below.

Step 1: Select the Industry

For the business analyst, selecting the industry for analysis is straightforward. For the all-source analyst, however, selecting the region or country of strategic interest is even more straightforward. If a nation wants to foster development of an industry with a view toward improving national competitiveness, its domestic firms must become efficient producers of that industry's products. While a nation can subsidize an inefficient industry, that does not mean its segment of the industry will have a comparative advantage over another nation's industrial capability for that product. For the all-source analyst, the policy or resource actions by a nation in fostering development in their industrial capability are of interest for the strategic intelligence insights they may provide.

Criteria for Selecting Industry

Our selection criteria include looking for an industry that is mature, global, and has a large presence in the region or country we are interested in. But first, a couple of new terms—*mature* and *global*—require a brief explanation.

The concept of industry *maturity* is sometimes shown as a stage in the life cycle of an industry. Using the measure of industry sales, the industry life cycle has the following periods: introduction, growth, maturity, and decline.[36] Other industry life-cycle portrayals, using the same measure of industry sales, label the periods of change as fragmentation, shakeout, maturity, and decline.[37] For our analysis, a mature industry is one in which the industry structure is stable and there is little change in the rank of leading firms.

A *global* industry is where an individual firm's competitive position in one country is affected by its position in other countries, and the reverse is also true.[38]

The final criterion, a large presence in the region or country, provides a starting point in selecting and reviewing industry candidates. Potential candidates for industry analysis are available from reviewing the Department of Commerce website for publicly released analysis on U.S. International Trade in Goods and Services. For this example, Department of Commerce International Trade Administration (ITA) publicly released factsheets were used.[39] A March 2009 ITA factsheet states that "capital goods" represent the largest U.S. export category and lists the top capital good export categories as civilian aircraft ($3.8 billion), semiconductors ($2.6 billion), industrial machines ($2.3 billion), telecommunications equipment ($2.3 billion), and medicinal equipment ($2.2 billion).[40] The United States holds a comparative advantage in these industries, where we are the more efficient producer of a product and it is to the advantage of other nations to trade with us to obtain that product or service. Conversely, a list of major U.S. *imports* would indicate where other nations' industries may have a comparative advantage over U.S. industry.

Starting with the ITA export factsheet cited earlier, an Internet search for the worldwide manufacturing rankings for an industry will provide a quick check on that industry's presence in the region or country of interest. This Internet search will also provide initial leads on sources of information regarding the industry.

To illustrate our analysis, the semiconductor industry will be the industry analysis example for the remaining steps. The semiconductor industry is a major export for the United States. It is a *mature* industry with established leaders, and a *global* industry with major outsourcing of manufacturing steps, such that any changes that affect facilities in other countries have an effect throughout a firm's operations. Other countries in the world want to advance in this industry, so industry analysis may yield strategic intelligence insights into another nation's plans and intentions that may affect U.S. comparative advantage in the semiconductor industry and, by extension, U.S. national competitiveness. Finally, the semiconductor industry has a large presence in East Asia, a region of strategic intelligence interest to the United States.

USING INDUSTRY ANALYSIS FOR STRATEGIC INTELLIGENCE

Step 2: Define the Industry

The starting point for the business analyst in formulating industry strategies and plans is to first define the industry and understand its structure. The importance of specifically identifying the industry for analysis is analogous to the task of the all-source analyst in clearly identifying collections requirements. In business, the analyst may have the subject-matter advantage of being in the industry, but there are still limits on the resources available for collection and analysis. The analyst in business may start with the six-digit North American Industry Classification System (NAICS) code for his or her industry and use it to access industry data collected by the U.S. Department of Commerce.[41] While the NAICS code and Department of Commerce data are available to the all-source analyst as well, the ITA factsheet and Internet search results that the previous step provides are more germane to that analyst.

To understand the industry under analysis, the all-source analyst has to research sources of general information on semiconductors and the industry. Appendix B provides the results of open-source Internet research on the basics of semiconductors and their manufacture.

Constructing a Value Chain: Aid to Industry Definition

One way to capture an understanding of this newfound information is to construct a value chain for the industry. The following discussion on developing an industry value chain is based on the information in Appendix B.

An industry value chain is the set of interrelated activities that, taken together, cover the cost of providing the product or service. For the semiconductor industry, the standardization of process steps and information exchange between processing steps led to the globalization of the value chain for this mature industry.[42] The semiconductor or electronic components industry and the term "value chain" are mentioned frequently in academic and industry trade journals. There are even illustrations of value chains for various aspects of the semiconductor industry available on the Internet. For example, in Figure 3.1, the Taiwan Semiconductor Industry Association 2009 Report outlines a semiconductor value chain to indicate the number and distribution of Taiwan firms comprised in its domestic semiconductor industry.

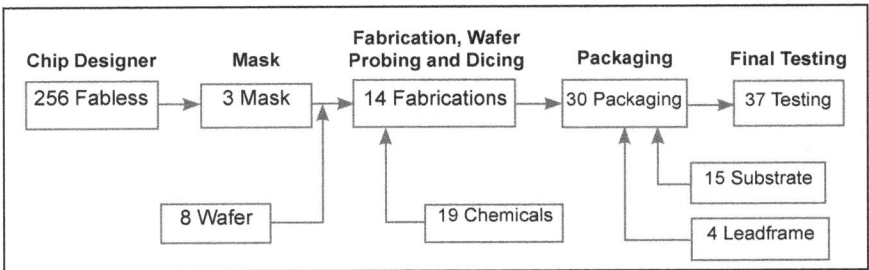

Figure 3.1: Taiwan Semiconductor Industry, 2008 (© Taiwan Semiconductor Industry Association)[43]

The Taiwan semiconductor industry value chain follows the product flow from design to test of the packaged chip. The figure indicates that, in 2008, Taiwan had 256 firms involved in the design of integrated circuits. The term "fabless" denotes firms that create and sell the designs of integrated circuits, but do not fabricate (manufacture) integrated circuits. The figure also indicates 14 firms with fabrication operations and 30 firms with packaging operations.

Academic papers employ value chains to evaluate industries, and those value chains produced in the country of interest can yield insights into how important an industry is to a nation. For example, Figure 3.2 shows a semiconductor value chain reflecting Taiwan's capability in the design of integrated circuits relative to capabilities of other advanced countries. The *Technovation* article from which the figure was derived goes on to discuss the strategy of the Taiwan semiconductor industry and the reasons behind its relative success at that point in time. Although dated, the article still provides background for collection and analysis on the semiconductor industry in Taiwan.

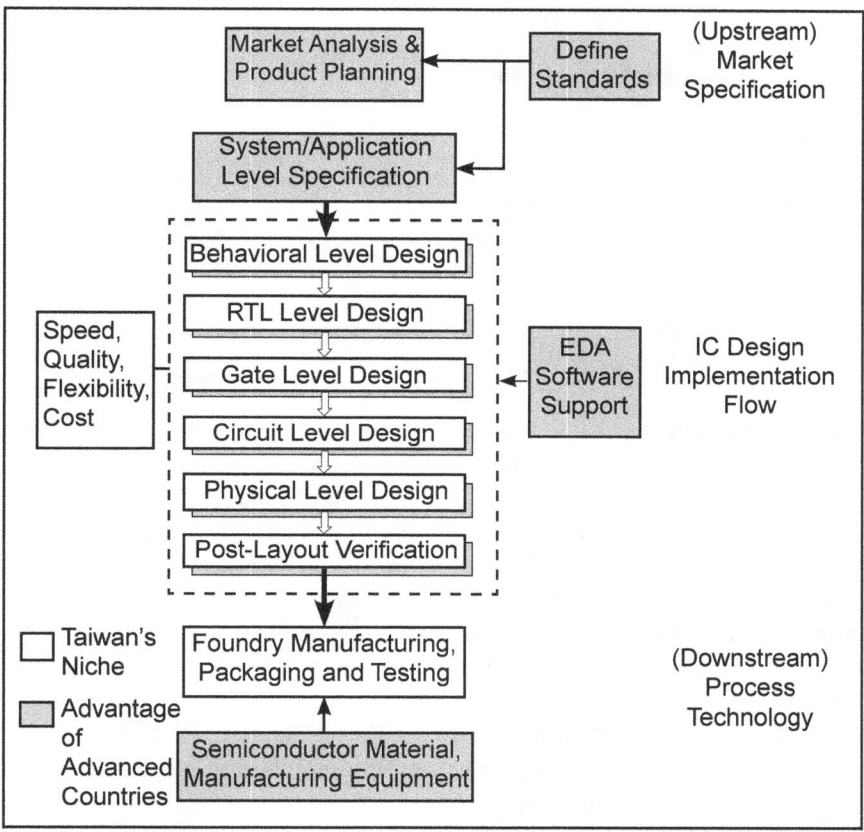

Figure 3.2: Taiwan Integrated Circuit Design Capabilities (© Elsevier)[44]

For our immediate purposes, the value chain in Figure 3.2 confirms the steps and their sequence in the production of semiconductors. The value chain also provides key terms that are encountered in analyzing the semiconductor industry.

Figure 3.3 shows a semiconductor value chain that can be used to illustrate the semiconductor manufacturing process and the globalization of the industry value chain.

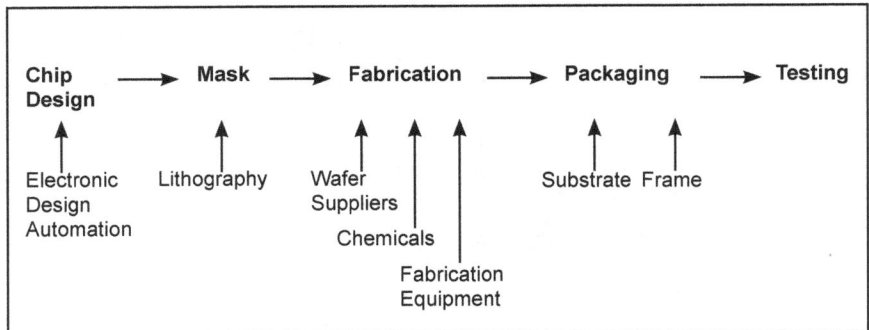

Figure 3.3: Semiconductor Value Chain[45]

Figure 3.3 shows the major value-added activities in the industry (chip design, mask, etc.), as well as the key suppliers to the industry (electronic design automation, lithography, etc.). An important point for analysts to understand is the variation in ownership of the value-chain activities for this mature industry. For example, in Figure 3.4, the top value chain shows the domain of the integrated design manufacturer and refers to a firm that participates in all the steps in the value chain. In terms of global value-chain governance (remember Figure 2.5), this is a hierarchical governance with high degrees of explicit coordination within the firm and power asymmetry over the suppliers. The middle value chain in Figure 3.4 shows the domain of the foundry, and refers to a semiconductor fabrication firm that fabricates the wafers from designs provided by other firms, and then returns the wafers to the customer. Finally, the bottom value chain in Figure 3.4 shows the domain of a fabless firm. This firm creates the integrated circuit design (intellectual property) and sells the design to other companies or subcontracts for fabrication.

In terms of global value-chain governance, both a foundry and a fabless firm are examples of modular value-chain governance. The standardization of design-manufacturing interfaces and information supports a lower degree of explicit coordination and power asymmetry over others. A useful way to think of power asymmetry is in terms of the power of the buyer or supplier in the interchange. The integrated design manufacturer has a lot more power over suppliers than the foundry or fabless firm.

USING INDUSTRY ANALYSIS FOR STRATEGIC INTELLIGENCE

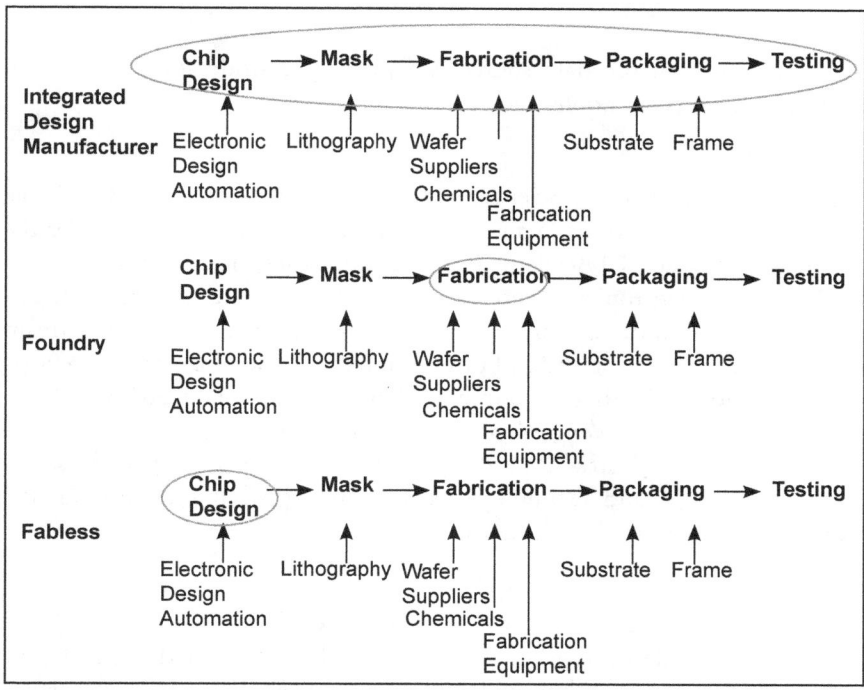

Figure 3.4: Semiconductor Value Chain—Firm Participation[46]

Step 3: Identify Sources of Information

Timothy Sturgeon points out the importance of not focusing on macro-level statistics, such as trade and investment, to understand a country's plans and intentions, because they "cannot help but render invisible the detailed contours of the world economy."[47] Also beware the technophile's focus on "the next big thing" or, at the other end of the spectrum, the engineer's focus on details. Keep these cautions in mind when starting to scan and select topics from the "daily scrape" for further review and analysis.[48]

This section takes the next step of identifying the types of potential open-source data available to support the industry analysis. Appendix C lists, by category, potential data sources specific to the semiconductor industry.

Books

While currency of the data source is a primary consideration, the search should include recent books on the industry.

Reports

The National Academy of Sciences, a nonprofit institution, has a searchable website of its publications, many of which are free to download. While the publication of National Academy reports is unpredictable, you can set e-mail notifications when topics of interest are available. The federal government, particularly within the Department of Commerce, provides a regular stream of trade and industry statistics, but occasionally it will also produce reports on global trade topics that are of interest. For example, the Bureau of Industry and Security (*www.bis.doc.gov/*) provides current news regarding trade issues, and the Defense Industrial Base Programs link provides a list of Defense Industrial Capability and Technology Assessments regarding foreign industrial development that may be of interest.

Trade Associations

Most industries have trade associations, and the associations usually release publications. Trade association websites provide news and documents, although the frequency of their updates and data available can be irregular.

Trade Journals

The most useful sources of current information are the industry trade journals. While there are government policy announcements and occasional analytical articles of use in metropolitan newspapers and business magazines, many of the stories are not much more than news releases from the subject company.

Other Internet Sources

This category concerns the ever-evolving platforms and content of the Internet. A few examples follow.

YouTube

The website YouTube (*www.youtube.com*), although pedestrian to aficionados of social media, can still provide good sources of information.

USING INDUSTRY ANALYSIS FOR STRATEGIC INTELLIGENCE

Blogs

Blogs written by industry analysts, enthusiasts, or employees can be a good source of information.

Twitter

The use of Twitter by the trade journals and even companies is noteworthy, but they typically tweet links to journal or marketing content already accessible via other means.

Webcasts, Virtual Conferences

The increasing use of webcasts and virtual conferences are good real-time sources. Subscriptions to the industry trade journals will lead to announcements of these events. The events offer another avenue for the industry to share information and develop market opportunities. The presenter slides are usually available for download prior to the presentation or the site may allow archival access.

Trade Shows

Trade shows, the best alternative to actually visiting semiconductor companies in other countries, obviously present challenges to the all-source analyst even beyond the requirements of time and funding. Trade association websites and trade journals carry advertisements for upcoming tradeshows. Tradeshows offer sessions in a variety of areas; it pays to read the program beforehand to ensure that the tradeshow is not devoted to a sub-industry topic or technical interchange. Also, unless the analyst is multilingual, it is advisable to ensure that the session is in English or a simultaneous translation is available. A walkthrough of the exhibit halls, including gathering literature, proves useful. One caution is that most corporate booths require a business card or the signing of a register before they provide literature. The purpose of the exhibit hall is to generate business leads for the companies, so the collection of literature may have to be skipped if identification presents a problem.

Step 4: Collect Information

For the purposes of this discussion, data was collected from November 2009 to June 2010, using all of the sources discussed in the preceding subsection. The sources included subscriptions to multiple semiconductor industry trade journals, two semiconductor industry trade shows (Tokyo and Seoul), and one industry strategy symposium (Half Moon Bay, California). With the Porter Five Forces and the Value Chain Models for context, relevant online information was saved in the program Zotero, organized by folders labeled with the External Environment Model segments. Also available were digital copies of the tradeshow proceedings.

Preparing for Collection

The sources that are included in the "daily scrape" of open-source media require preplanning.

Using E-mail as an Information Portal

For this project, a separate Gmail account was created just to receive industry trade journals and other industry source materials. During the workweek, the trade journals push their content out to subscribers. Via the Gmail account, it was possible to quickly scan the subjects and synopsis of articles in each journal.

Capturing and Sorting Information

There are several ways to capture results. One approach is to use a series of e-mail folders to keep and organize items of interest. The freeware program Zotero was chosen to collect, manage, and cite the source materials.[49] Zotero was active and ready to use whenever the browser was open. Saving a copy of an article entailed clicking the Zotero icon in the toolbar, and selecting "create new item" in the folder designated. Zotero uses a cloud-based storage approach to capture a copy of the specific article, and also puts a copy on the computer. The reviewed trade journal is placed in a folder within the Gmail account that is marked by the name of the journal in case it is necessary to access the journal again. The advantage of Zotero's cloud-based approach is that the analyst can work from multiple computers and keep up with the work. In June 2010, Zotero's annual rate was $20 for 1 GB of storage ($1.67 per month). A plus for Zotero is that it has a plug-in to Microsoft Word, permitting direct transfer of citations from Zotero to a Word document.[50]

USING INDUSTRY ANALYSIS FOR STRATEGIC INTELLIGENCE

Filing Information

The External Environment Model provided the framework for active collection of information on the industry. Folders were created in Zotero and labeled with the names of the segments in the model. Here is the list of virtual folders established in Zotero to capture information:

Demographics
Economic
Global
- *China*
- *Europe*
- *India*
- *Japan*
- *Korea*
- *Singapore*
- *Taiwan*

Political/Legal

Sociocultural

Technological

Note that, within the global element, country-specific folders were also developed for information that pertains only to that country. There is also a folder named Industry Analysis that was used to collect information regarding the structure and conduct of the industry. Figure 3.5 shows a screenshot of the online data collection (Zotero tool) for this industry analysis.

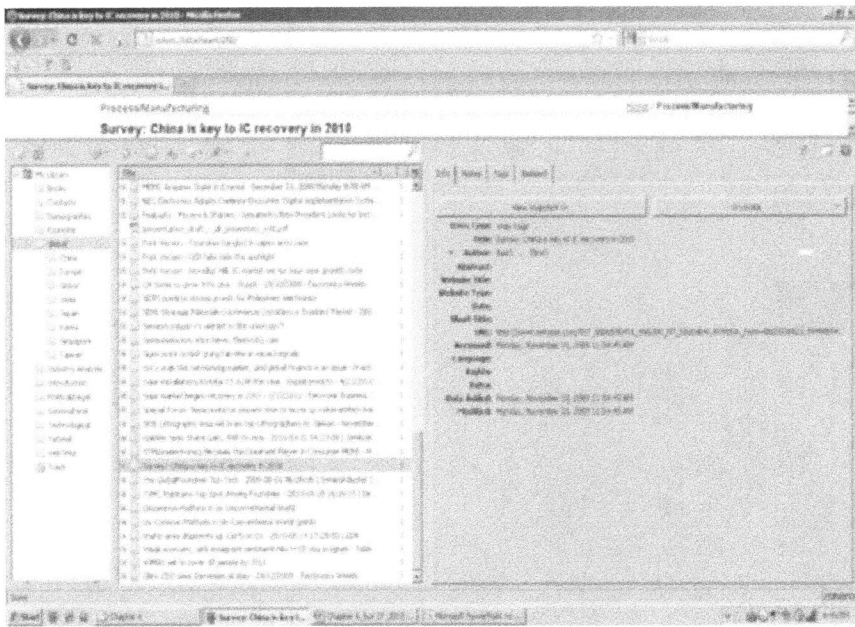

Figure 3.5: Data Collection Using Zotero

In Figure 3.5, the Global folder is highlighted in the far-left column. The middle column lists all the articles saved in that Global folder; highlighted is an article titled "Survey: China is key to IC recovery in 2010." Double-clicking on that title opens up the article in that window for rereading. In the far-right column is a snapshot of the citation, including the date it was accessed and the article's Web address. The review and collection of data in one place with a clear documentation trail will be advantageous during the analysis. Once the data-collection framework is in place, the analyst can start reviewing and collecting information. There will be a large volume of information arriving every day, but it is possible to quickly scan and save information of interest.

Industry Observations from Data Collection

Thus far, we have discussed the first four steps: select the industry; define the industry; identify sources of information; and collect information. In this

USING INDUSTRY ANALYSIS FOR STRATEGIC INTELLIGENCE

subsection, we look at industry observations resulting from the data collection. We summarize observations on the current state of the semiconductor industry based on the results of the open-source collection. The summary will provide a backdrop for step five: analyze results (the following subsection). There, we will review and analyze collection results on East Asia—the focus of our analysis.

At this point, the analyst should be comfortable with reviewing incoming information on the semiconductor industry. The Five Forces Model and the Value Chain Model aid in reading and comprehension during collection. The External Environment Model and the Zotero software tool provide a means to sort and preserve collection results. The observations at this point will be a collection of opinions and facts consistent with how the industry views itself. While the psychology of intelligence analysis is beyond the scope of this discussion, Figure 3.6 provides a conceptual view of applying the industry analysis model for intelligence analysts.[51]

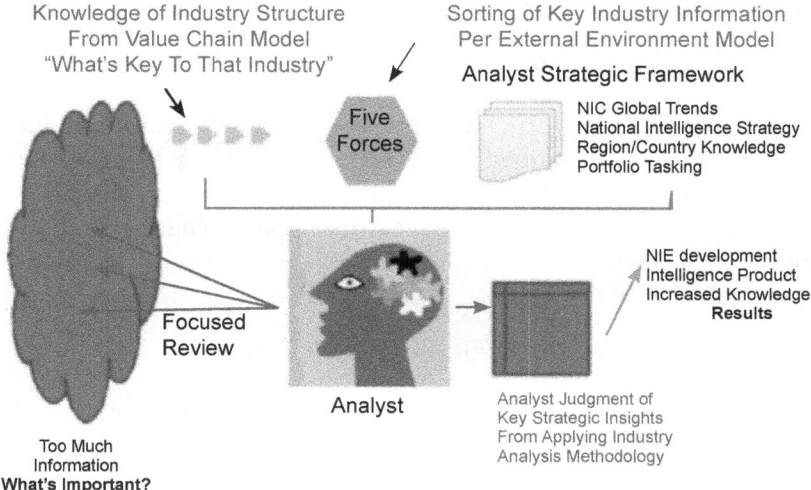

Figure 3.6: Conceptual View of Model Application

Figure 3.6 shows the analyst at the center because he or she is the target audience for this book. On the left side, the blue cloud indicates the large amount of open-source information and the caption "Too Much Information" describes the daily challenge of the all-source analyst. Along the top are arrayed the various models described in Chapter 2, but it also includes the analyst's strategic perspective and tradecraft experience. The combination of industry analysis models and the strategic framework provides a new lens for the analyst to now perform a "Focused Review" of industry-related data. The "Analyst Judgment of Key Strategic Intelligence Insights" represents the intellectual task of reviewing and assessing the information collected. This is not a serial process; the analyst over time builds a strategic perspective of the industry and draws equally strategic and intelligence insights (or connections) from his or her tradecraft experience. This subsection provides the result of building a strategic perspective on the semiconductor industry. Later in this chapter, under step 5, we describe the result of focusing our newfound perspective on the target region of East Asia and suggest strategic intelligence insights for use in the intelligence products listed in Figure 3.6 as "Results." It is worth stating again that the intellectual process of learning to use the industry analysis models, learning to understand the industry, collecting information, developing observations, and finally generating strategic intelligence insights is not serial.

Summary of Industry Observations

The semiconductor industry faces continuing consumer demand to increase capability and decrease prices. The advances in technology have been impressive; however, achieving each advancement (sometimes referred to as a technology "node") requires enormous amounts of capital, and it is the economics, not the technology, that is becoming the main driver. Four primary observations resulted from the information collection and analysis of the industry:

1. Economics of pursuing the leading edge is in question;

2. "Globalization" of the industry market is not a remedy for profitability concerns;

3. East Asia's emergence as the industry's production center is an outcome of pursuing profitability through globalization; and

4. Industry's active pursuit of alternative markets for avenues of profitability is an outgrowth of the competitiveness within the industry.

USING INDUSTRY ANALYSIS FOR STRATEGIC INTELLIGENCE

Economics of Pursuing Leading Edge Is in Question

A hallmark achievement of this industry has been its ability to regularly deliver increasing capability. However, while there is a lot of discussion of the approaching physical limits of achieving further increases in the number of transistors that can be crammed onto an integrated circuit, industry analysts believe the real barrier may be an economic one. At semiconductor equipment conferences this year, several speakers brought up the point that new technology nodes may not meet the 18-month cycle of delivering new capability per Moore's Law.[52] Figure 3.7 illustrates the industry's fear that the financial hurdles may be too great for delivering new capability.

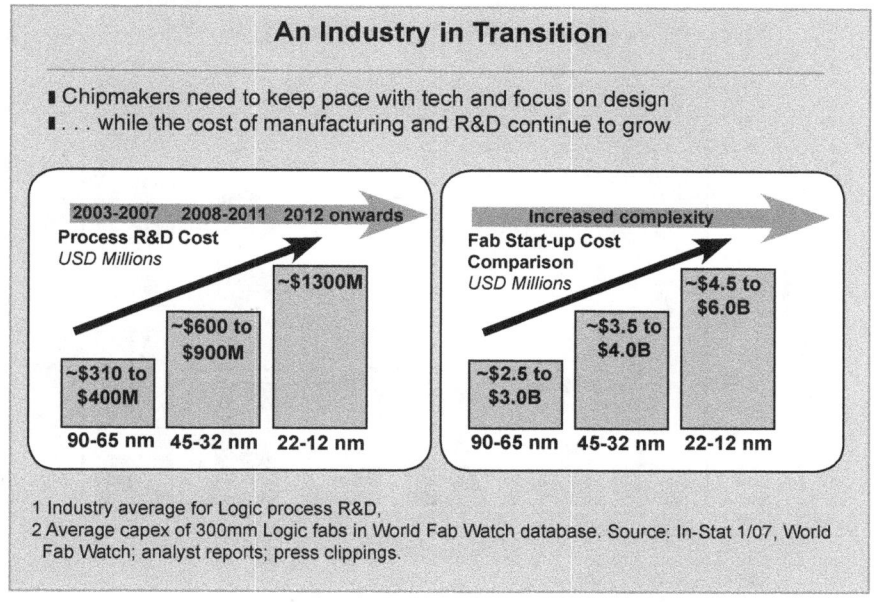

Figure 3.7: Financial Hurdles for Semiconductor Industry (© GLOBALFOUNDRIES)[53]

Figure 3.7 shows the increasing research and development costs required to achieve decreasing feature size. The figure also shows that the industry faces huge costs to build the fabrication facility to render that design into a chip. In terms of Porter's Five Forces Model, both of these factors represent high barriers to entry for a company interested in joining the industry. These large investments also represent high exit costs for existing firms.

Figures 3.8 and 3.9 illustrate that even the *conceptualization* and *design* of leading-edge chips are becoming cost prohibitive and resulting in fewer new design starts. One result is that many companies within the industry will continue production using older feature dimensions, and will reuse old blocks of design (intellectual property) in order to avoid the enormous costs of leading-edge design and fabrication.

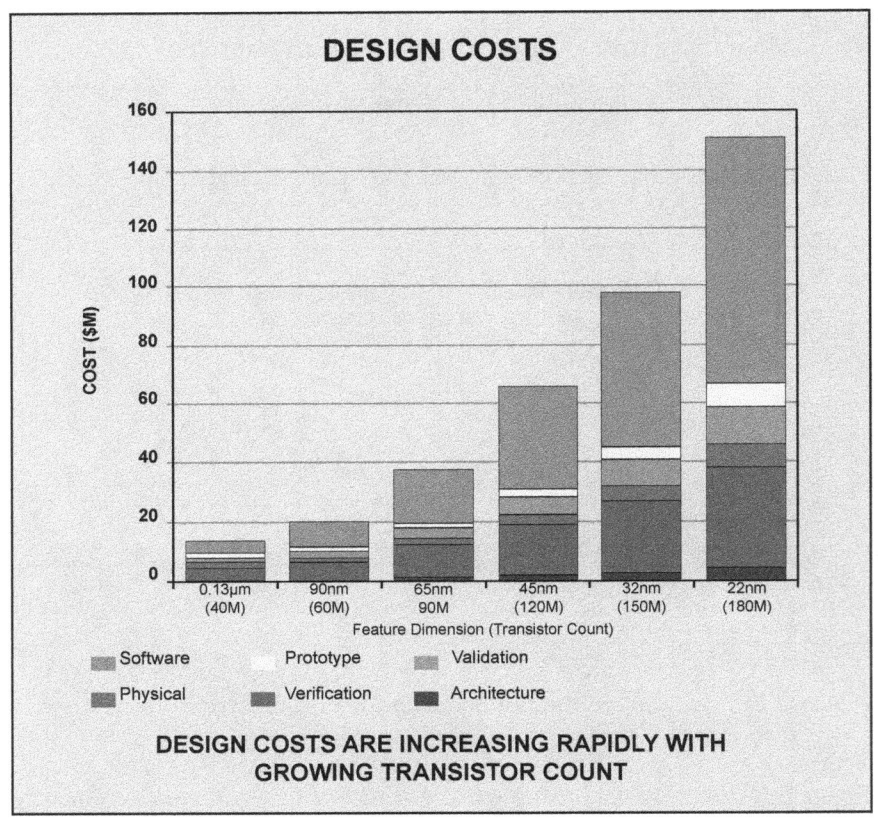

Figure 3.8: Increasing Design Costs (© International Business Strategies, Inc.)[54]

USING INDUSTRY ANALYSIS FOR STRATEGIC INTELLIGENCE

Figure 3.8 illustrates the increasing cost of design in leading-edge integrated circuits. The growing software cost is due to the increase in software required throughout the design process to achieve breakthroughs in the performance of integrated circuits.

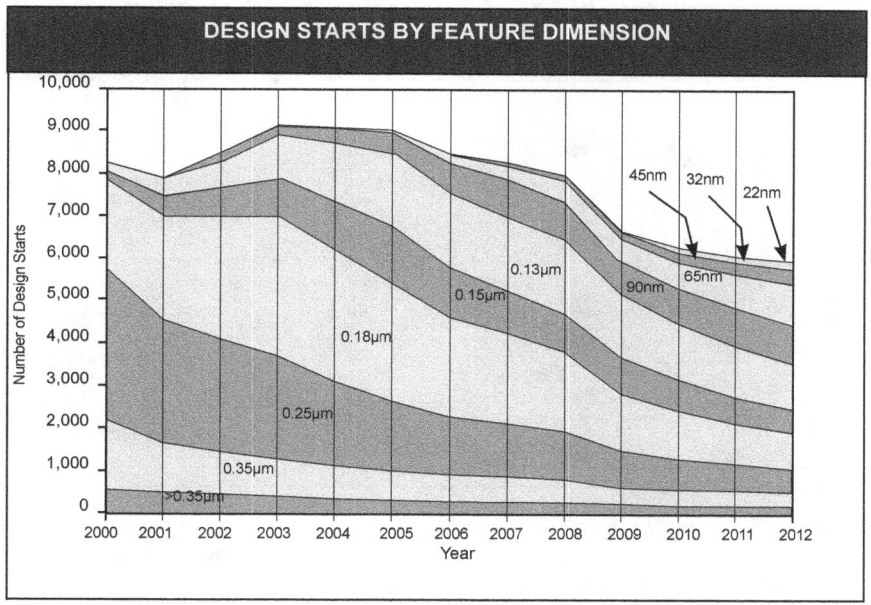

Figure 3.9: Decreasing Design Starts (© International Business Strategies, Inc., 2010)[55]

Figure 3.9 illustrates that increasing costs of pursuing the leading edge in semiconductors are resulting in a slowdown of new starts in leading-edge design. Instead, companies are trying to earn as much revenue as possible from existing designs and fabrication facilities. In terms of the Five Forces Model, the intensity of competition requires a company to commit huge amounts of capital in order to stay at the leading edge of the industry. These capital commitments have led to fewer competitors with clear leaders in each category of the industry. For example, Intel is the world leader in microprocessor units in terms of sales and market share.

When you factor in the huge costs to stay on the leading edge and the industry's claim that the returns on investment are increasingly difficult to find, it is hard to see why firms even try to pursue the leading edge. Figure 3.10 shows a slide from an industry strategy session that graphically captures this point, but does not provide any answers.

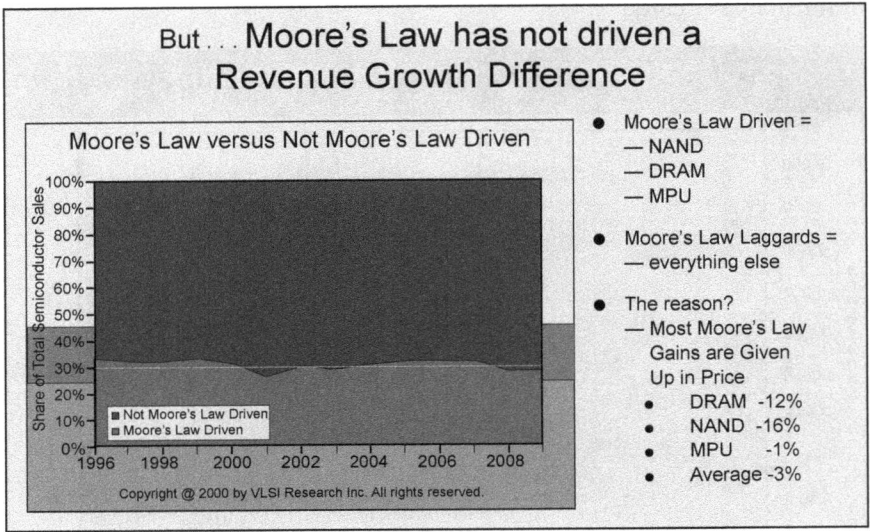

Figure 3.10: Lagging Edge over Leading Edge in Semiconductor Sales (© VLSIresearch. "Economics and Collaboration Panel Discussion" SEMI ISS 2010. Half Moon Bay: SEMI, 2010.)[56]

Figure 3.10 illustrates that, despite all the attention paid to the leading edge (Moore's Law–driven) and the expectation that a leading-edge strategy will result in higher profits, the fact is that the share of total semiconductor sales has remained steady between the leading and lagging edge. The statement "Most Moore's Law Gains are Given Up in Price" illustrates the power of the buyer (in this case, the electronics-equipment manufacturer) in the semiconductor industry. So the semiconductor firm (supplier) has to either find ways to remain competitive or exit the industry, possibly going out of business altogether.

Unfortunately, even if a company steps back from the enormous costs of leading-edge fabrication, it will still face intense price competition in the trailing edge that requires it to carefully select its strategy. Figure 3.11 shows that, while integrated design manufacturers still predominated in the top 20 semiconductor sales leaders (as of 2008), the Taiwan Semiconductor Manufacturing Company, a *pure-play foundry*, is in the top five, and two *fabless*

USING INDUSTRY ANALYSIS FOR STRATEGIC INTELLIGENCE

firms, Qualcomm and Broadcom, registered the highest growth rates. For the remaining integrated design manufacturers to stay at the leading edge, they must continue to leverage their lead in market segments with large amounts of capital investment.

2008 Top 20 Semiconductor Sales Leaders ($M)						
2008 Rank	2007 Rank	Company	Headquarters	2007 Tot Semi	2008 Tot Semi	2008/2007 % Change
1	1	Intel	U.S.	35,021	34,490	-2%
2	2	Samsung	South Korea	19,951	20,272	2%
3	3	TI	U.S.	13,309	11,966	-10%
4	4	Toshiba	Japan	11,850	11,059	-7%
5	5	TSMC*	Taiwan	9,813	10,556	8%
6	7	ST**	Europe	8,637	9,052	5%
7	8	Renesas	Japan	8,001	7,017	-12%
8	13	Qualcomm***	U.S.	5,619	6,477	15%
9	9	Sony	Japan	7,203	6,420	-11%
10	6	Hynix	South Korea	9,201	6,182	-33%
11	12	Infineon	Europe	5,772	5,972	3%
12	11	AMD	U.S.	6,013	5,808	-3%
13	14	NEC	Japan	5,593	5,732	2%
14	15	Micron	U.S.	5,520	5,688	3%
15	10	NXP	Europe	6,026	5,318	-12%
16	16	Freescale	U.S.	5,447	4,898	-10%
17	23	Broadcom***	U.S.	3,754	4,509	20%
18	17	Fujitsu	Japan	4,568	4,462	-2%
19	21	Panasonic	Japan	3,810	4,321	13%
20	19	Nvidia***	U.S.	3,979	3,660	-8%
--	--	Total Top 20	--	179,087	173,859	-3%

*Foundry   **Not incl. flash and ST-NXP Wireless in 2007 & 2008   ***Fabless
Source: Company reports, IC Insights

Figure 3.11: Integrated Design Manufacturers Still Predominate (© IC Insights)[57]

Figure 3.11 not only lists the leaders in the semiconductor industry, it also shows the international makeup of the industry. One notable absence on the list is mainland China, which is usually portrayed in the media as a juggernaut in manufacturing.

"Globalization" of the Industry Market is not a Remedy for Profitability Concerns

Collaboration and Protection of Intellectual Property

The industry understands the technology challenges ahead, but finds it increasingly difficult to find the capital and business model to fund the necessary research and development for pursuit of the next technology node. One possible solution the industry is exploring is collaborations in research and development between semiconductor firms. The International Semiconductor Technology Roadmap is the best example of this type of collaboration. Participating firms are able to share technology and still achieve differentiation in their product.

A few large firms, such as Intel, still choose to fund their own research and development and keep their technology advantage in-house. Other firms also carefully guard their intellectual property, but do so in a surprising way. For example, within weeks of the release of Apple's iPad, the Canadian company Chipworks released an analysis and cross-section images of the core processor chip and correctly identified Samsung as the designer and fabricator.[58] This practice of reverse engineering and publishing the integrated circuit design of another firm is protected by the Semiconductor Chip Protection Act in the United States, which allows reverse engineering "for the purpose of teaching, analyzing, or evaluating the concepts or techniques embodied in the mask work or circuitry."[59] The industry uses this carefully stipulated openness to share achievements and protect its intellectual property.

Expanding Market, Increasing Competition

Another hallmark of this industry is the growth in unit volume, which drives lower cost per unit of semiconductors. One observation in *EE Times India* stated that "the total semiconductor TAM [total available market] grows because of—not in spite of—the 35 percent per year reduction in the unit price of transistors."[60]

During this past decade, electronics consumption has shifted from business use to personal and home use, and this is growing despite the economic downturn. One supporting figure cited is that 55 percent of the world GDP of electronics is now from personal consumption.[61] The $226 billion semiconductor industry is a key part of the $1.1 trillion electronics industry.[62] Despite the recent economic downturn, the semiconductor content of electronic systems was forecasted to increase about 27 percent for 2010.[63]

A major portent of the future of the semiconductor market lies in the rising awareness of people in other parts of the world to the use of portable electronics such as cell phones. However, a significant portion of these groups only has an annual per capita income of greater than U.S. $3,000.[64] Industry analysts are warning business to be aware of the tipping point, when 50 percent or more of its demand is in emerging markets.[65] Figure 3.12 illustrates the point that, while the majority of this rising consumer class will have high expectations for capability, they will not have the economic means to afford it, thereby exerting further downward pressure on prices.

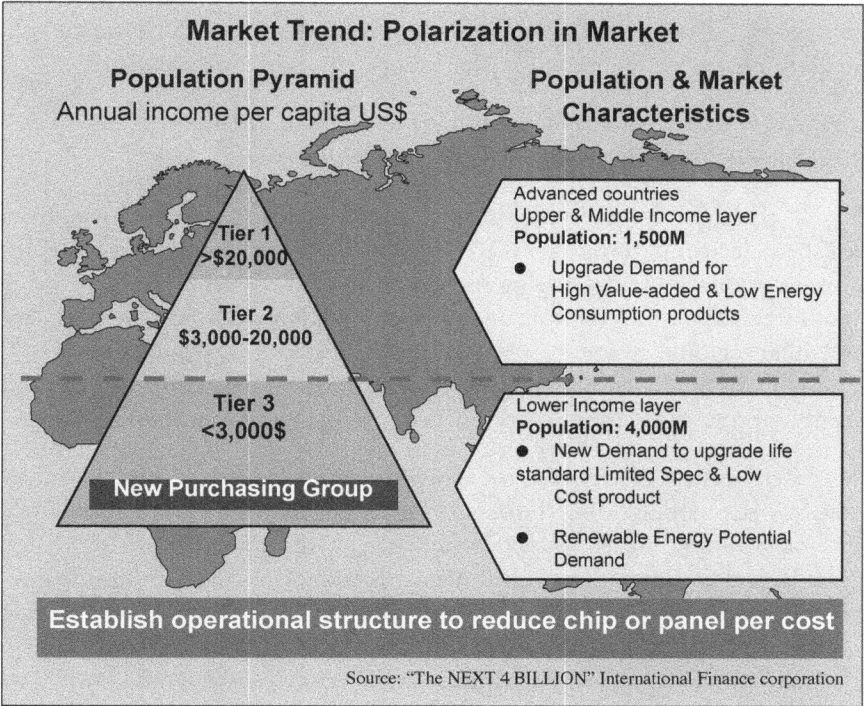

Figure 3.12: Future Market Economics (© Tokyo Electron using information from "The NEXT 4 Billion" International Finance Corporation and "The Fortune at the Bottom of the Pyramid" Strategy + Business, no. 26: 2–14)[66]

Figure 3.12 also provides a sociocultural insight regarding rising living conditions in developing nations around the world. While the industry is struggling with future profitability, demand in developing countries is increasing. This bodes ill for the semiconductor industry, because the power to set prices is still firmly in favor of the consumer.

Ultimately, a semiconductor company has to turn a profit in order to survive in the industry. Turning a profit means being able to sell enough chips over what it cost to develop and produce them. One figure cited at an industry strategy session is that there needs to be a total available market of at least $2 billion in order to justify pursuing a 32 nm advanced chip design.[67] The qualifying 2013 product markets were listed as mobile phones, personal computers, video games, and televisions with set top boxes. The financial community expects that before a semiconductor company invests its capital in a project, the expected value from the project will cover its investment and, in addition, earn a higher return than alternative uses for that capital.

East Asia's Emergence as the Industry's Production Center is an Outcome of Pursuing Profitability through Globalization

It was the drive for profitability that forced U.S. firms to first outsource finished electronic components to Asia for use in producing end items for consumption.[68] The developing standardization of design-to-manufacturing interfaces helped the rise in technical sophistication of Asian countries, and now that region is becoming the fabrication center of this global industry.[69] The global Value Chain "modular" model discussed earlier in this chapter neatly captures the current semiconductor design and fabrication processes.

The establishment of the *dedicated foundry model* in Taiwan is central to understanding the modularity of the industry.[70] While there are variations in scope and organization, in its simplest form, the foundry receives the chip design "intellectual property" from a customer and produces wafers with the integrated circuits. The customer then takes the wafer and either finishes the process or outsources it to yet another firm, so they only handle sales of the finished chip. A pure-play foundry does not fabricate and market its own chips. Sometimes an integrated design manufacturer will contract out its excess production capacity to other firms and produce chips in their fab for them.

The dedicated foundry is a way to transfer portions of the huge costs (and technology risks) of semiconductor fabrication outside of the firm. Some "fab-lite" semiconductor companies are reducing their fabrication capabilities to cover only key technology areas and are relying on foundries for production of the remainder of their product portfolio. Other "fabless" firms have no fabrication capability and are concentrating on generating designs for fabrication or for sale to other companies.

The result of all these changes is a shift in semiconductor manufacturing to Asia, where the majority of the foundries are located. Figure 3.13 shows, by geographic region, the change in installed capacity (use of 200 mm equivalents allows inclusion of all wafer sizes) from 1995 to 2009; it also includes forecasts for 2010 and 2011. The center of gravity for this industry is clearly shifting to East Asia.

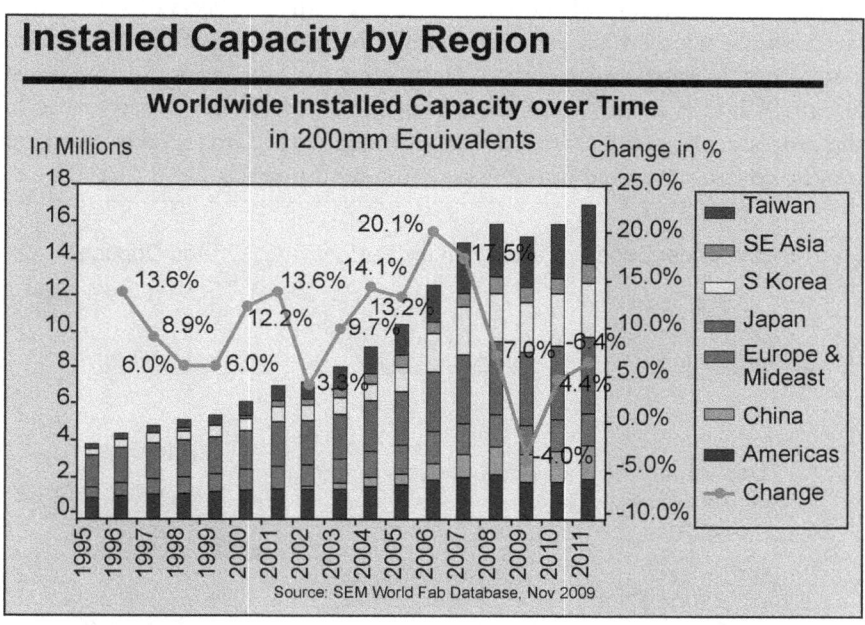

Figure 3.13: Rise of Asia in Semiconductor Manufacturing (© SEMI Industry Research & Statistics)[71]

Industry's Active Pursuit of Alternative Markets for Avenues of Profitability is an Outgrowth of the Competitiveness within the Industry

There are several promising areas for future growth in the semiconductor industry that are not as capital intensive or technologically challenging. These areas are photovoltaic (PV) and light emitting diodes (LED). There is also an emerging and potentially large application area for semiconductors in the biomedical market.

Photovoltaic (PV). Photovoltaic (or solar-cell) fabrication starts with square silicon wafers and uses a simpler—relative to CMOS (complementary metal-oxide-semiconductor)—fabrication process to produce a solar panel. Figure 3.14 shows a simplified version of the process; note the absence of the repeated mask exposures that produce the complex designs of an integrated circuit. The fabrication of the solar cell starts with flat sheets of silicon that are the same size as the finished solar cell. The processing of the silicon into a solar cell is much quicker than the process for fabricating an integrated circuit. While it is important to control the introduction of impurities in the process, solar-cell fabrication does not require the same level of stringent process controls involved in integrated-circuit fabrication.

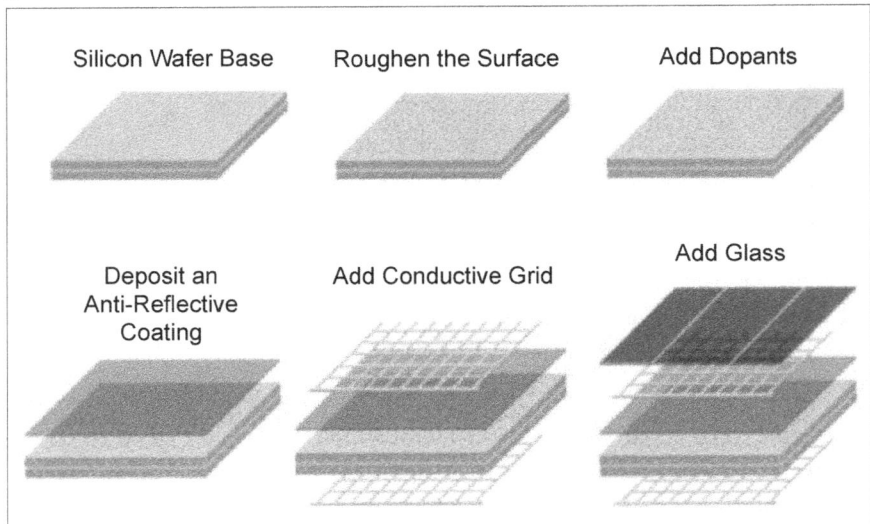

Figure 3.14: Fabrication of a Solar Cell[72]

USING INDUSTRY ANALYSIS FOR STRATEGIC INTELLIGENCE

The PV market is a topic of much discussion, but the business model for widespread adoption is still not in place. As Figure 3.15 indicates, demand in the industry is still heavily dependent on government subsidies for producers and consumers. Until PV can compete economically with conventional power sources, its progress will continue to depend on government subsidies.

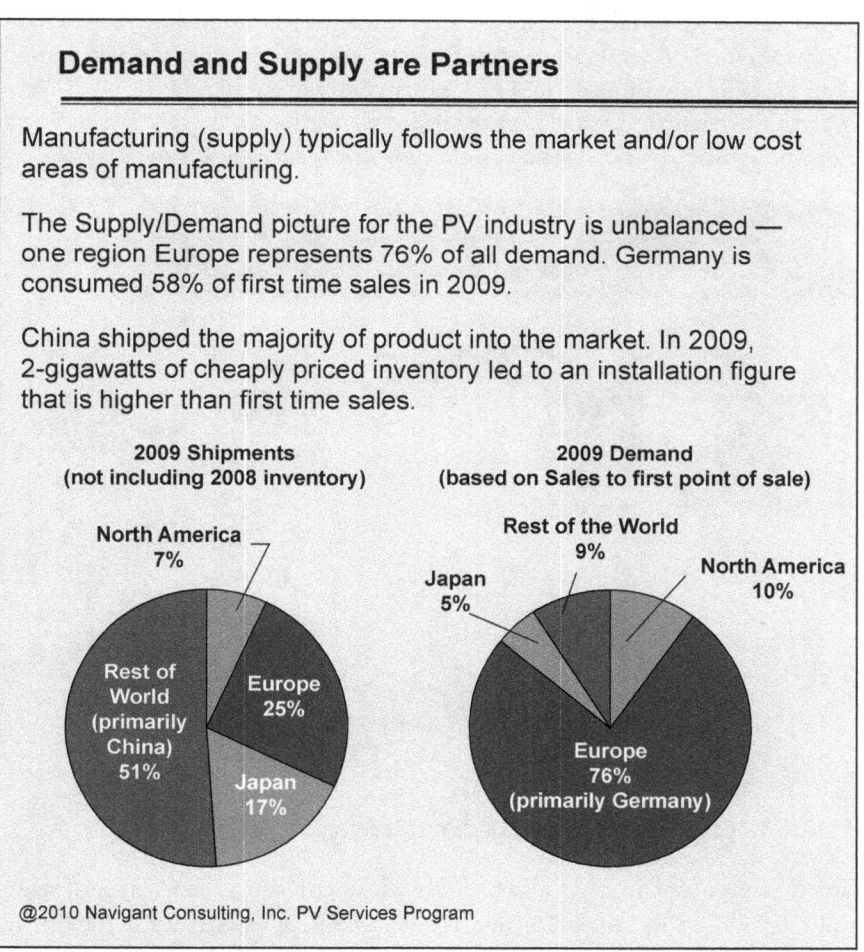

Figure 3.15: PV Market Still Developing (© Navigant Consulting)[73]

It is interesting to note from Figure 3.15 that China is a major producer of photovoltaic devices, but is not a major consumer. The fabrication finding is not surprising, since photovoltaic fabrication is not as complex as integrated circuits, but the future of mainland China as a consumer of photovoltaics remains open to speculation.

Light Emitting Diodes (LEDs). LEDs are another promising growth area. They are based on semiconductor substrates and, in concept, are even simpler than PV cells to produce. The LED industry is characterized as being 10 years behind the semiconductor industry in terms of process control and automation.[74] Figure 3.16 provides a simple view of the fabrication steps.

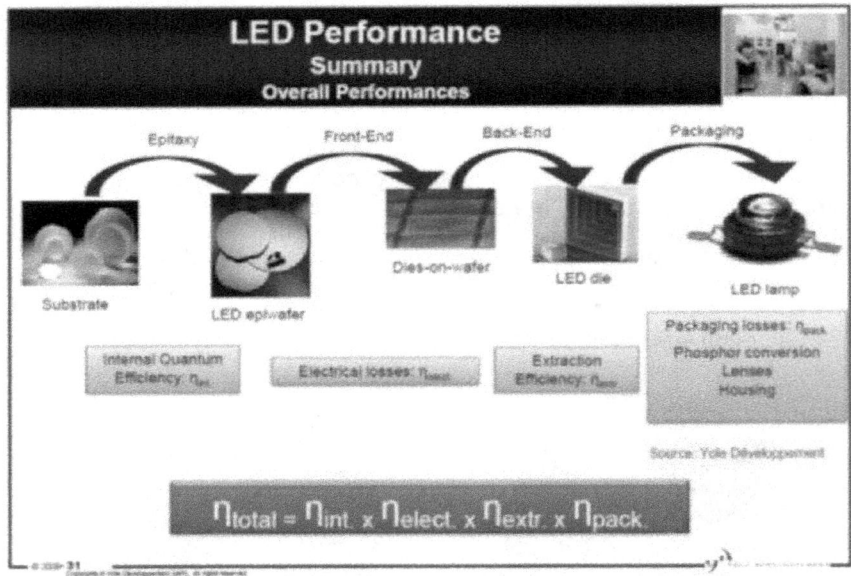

Figure 3.16: LED Fabrication (© Yole Développement)[75]

The fabrication of an LED also begins with silicon substrate. A layer of material is grown on the substrate, and the resulting epiwafer is ready for further processing. The dies are cut out of the epiwafer and packaged in a fixture with electrical connections.

Figure 3.17 shows that the promise of continuing market growth for LEDs is in the consumer-product areas of automobiles, flat-screen televisions and monitors, and energy-efficient applications, such as commercial and residential lighting. These growth projections and low technology barriers are now drawing larger semiconductor companies into this segment. While the consumer will benefit from the increasing competition, only the firms that can quickly scale up production will remain profitable.

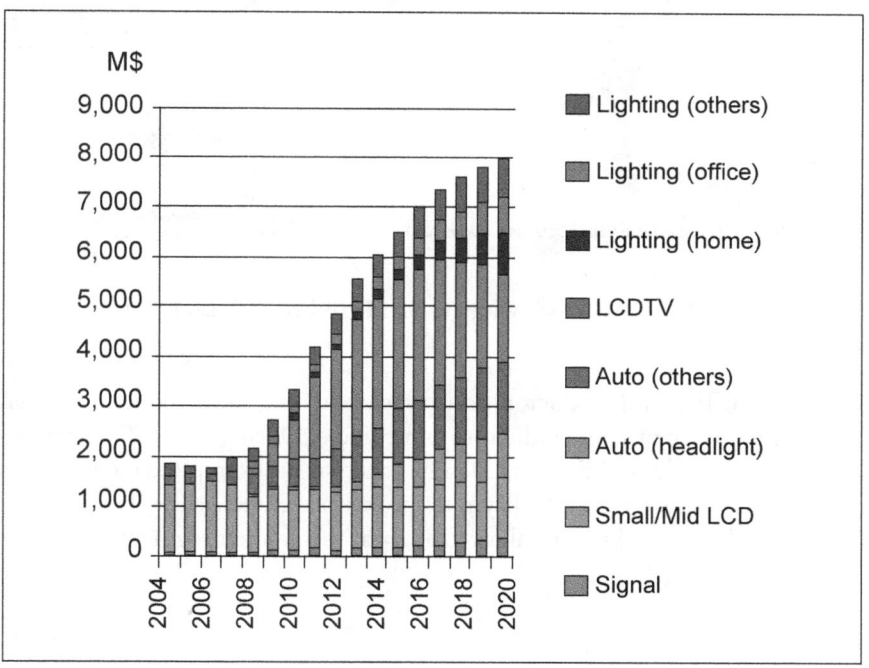

Figure 3.17: LED Market Forecast (© iSuppli)[76]

Figure 3.18 shows that the distribution of LED fabs is the highest in East Asia. The LED fab has a lower barrier to entry, and East Asia is close to the buyer (in this case, electronics and automotive manufacturers).

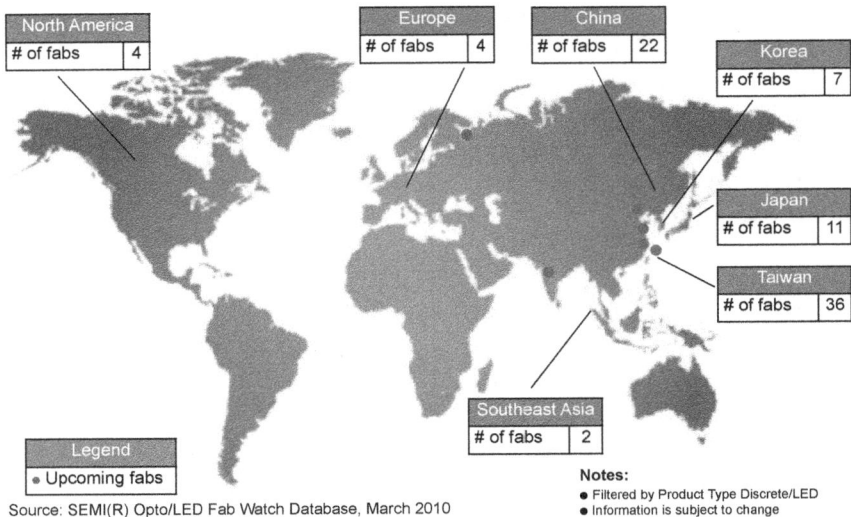

Figure 3.18: LED Fabs Worldwide (© SEMI Industry Research & Statistics)[77]

Biomedical. The semiconductor industry is awakening to the market potential of the application of semiconductors in medicine. During an *EE Times* virtual conference on Medical Systems Design (cited as an example data source in the preceding subsection), the keynote speaker presented a slide (Figure 3.19) listing the drivers and potential for growth in this market segment.

USING INDUSTRY ANALYSIS FOR STRATEGIC INTELLIGENCE

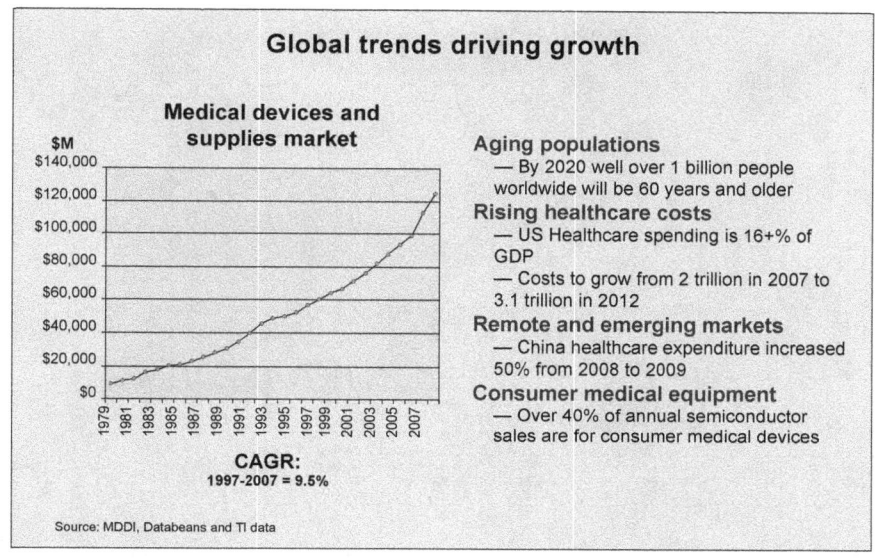

Figure 3.19: Medical Devices Market Potential (© Doug Rasor)[78]

Figure 3.19 provides insights into the drivers for potential demand for semiconductors in medical applications. The aging of populations in developing and developed nations is one driver. Another projected demand driver is rising healthcare costs, even in developing nations.

During a keynote address at SEMICON Korea, Tien Wu, the chief operating officer of ASE (Advanced Semiconductor Engineering), Taiwan (the world's largest provider of semiconductor-manufacturing services in assembly), presented a slide (Figure 3.20) showing that medical applications are part of the next semiconductor life cycle. The speaker went on to say that every single life cycle tends to be larger than the previous one, and champions of one tend to lose in the next life cycle.[79]

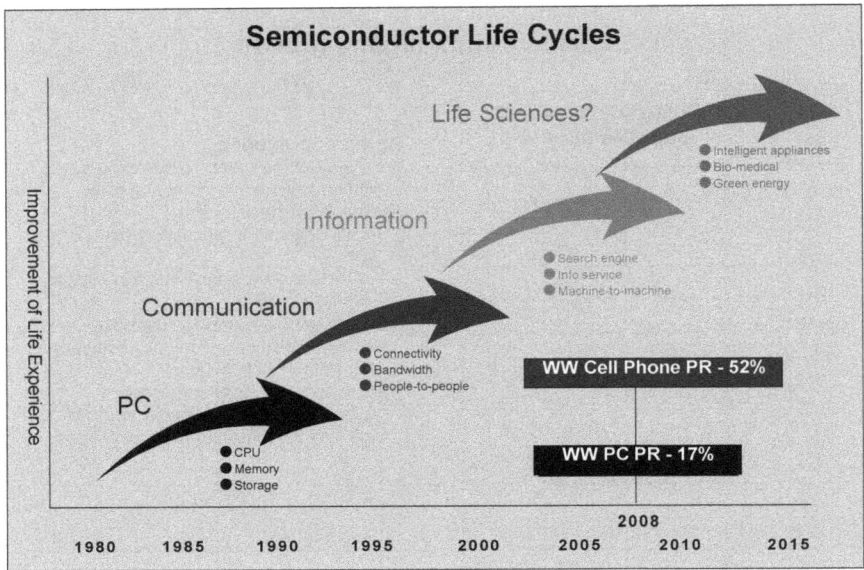

Figure 3.20: Semiconductor Life Cycles (© ASE Group)[80]

The continuing reductions in the size of integrated circuits and power requirements are raising the potential for integration of semiconductors into the human body. As Figure 3.21 illustrates, the applications of semiconductors are poised to become essential to our health and well-being.

USING INDUSTRY ANALYSIS FOR STRATEGIC INTELLIGENCE

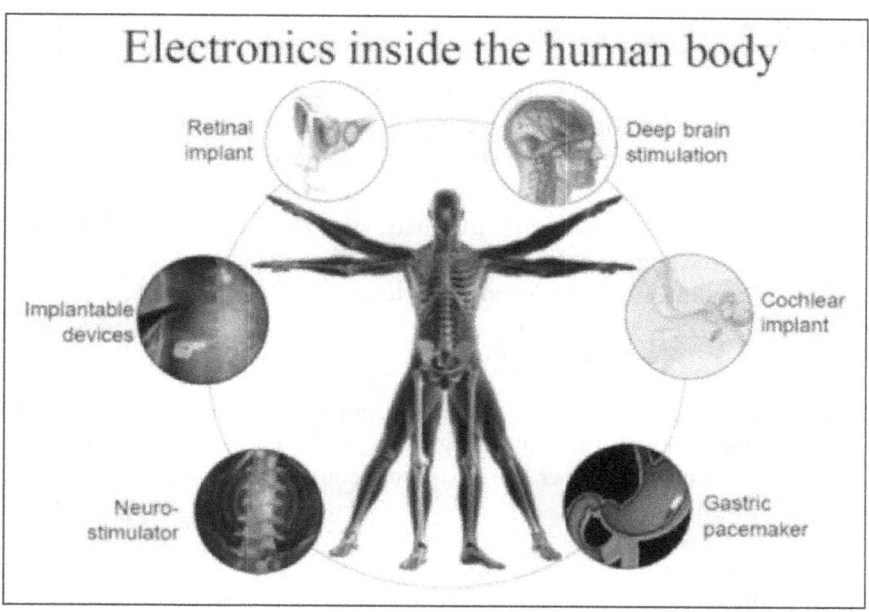

Figure 3.21: Semiconductor Integration into Biomedical Devices (© Doug Rasor)[81]

Summary

This subsection provided the result of building a strategic perspective on the semiconductor industry. The observations are the result of reviewing and evaluating a large body of collected information. The extensive footnoting for each observation provides the means for recalling and verifying the source of these observations. To summarize, particularly with respect to influences on the structure and conduct of relations between this industry and the governments with which they interact: (1) the industry is caught between buyer expectations and skyrocketing development and fabrication costs; (2) this industry-wide challenge at the leading edge is driving a continuing search for funding; and (3) the shakeout in the industry at the leading edge is driving competition in the trailing edge and alternate avenues of profitability (e.g., photovoltaic, LEDs, medical devices).

Step 5: Analyze Results

At this point, the all-source intelligence analyst needs to review the information collected and initial industry insights to make connections beyond the business world to produce strategic intelligence insights. The results of this fifth and final step will round out the all-source analysts' perspective and provide inputs for future intelligence products. We focus our newfound perspective on the target region of East Asia and suggest strategic intelligence insights for use in producing the intelligence products listed in Figure 3.6.

East Asia: Semiconductor Industry

While their approaches vary, the national governments in East Asia all set out to foster the establishment and growth of the industry.[82] But this governmental involvement does not guarantee continuing success. Brown and Linden explain:

> For governments, the years of U.S.-Japan rivalry established the reduced scope for government intervention in an established industry. In the 1970s a range of policy tools such as tariffs and subsidies were available to the Japanese government in its efforts to overtake U.S. chip firms, and international trade agreements forced these to be dropped once Japan's industry was established. The direct policy tools of the past have been sidelined by various agreements under the World Trade Organization (WTO), although developing countries like China are still able to provide subsidies to push their infant industry along.[83]

Figure 3.22 summarizes the state of the semiconductor industry in East Asia. A discussion of each country follows the figure.

USING INDUSTRY ANALYSIS FOR STRATEGIC INTELLIGENCE

	Market Strength	Value Chain Focus	Technology Node	Industry Outlook	Government Involvement	Observation
Japan	Memory	Lithography, Fabrication, Packaging, Testing	Leading Edge	Falling Behind ⬇	Minimal, Export Controls	Seeking growth through outsourcing and joint ventures in process R&D
Korea	Memory	Design, Fabrication, Packaging, Testing	Leading Edge	Memory ⬆	Trying to Expand Domestic Capability Beyond Memory Sector	One Company dominates. Domestic Industry is still developing.
Singapore	Foundry	Fabrication	TBD	TBD	TBD	Acquisition of Chartered by off-shore investors, outcome still TBD.
Taiwan	Memory, Foundry, PV, LED	Design, Fabrication, Packaging, Testing	Leading Edge	Positive Growth ⬆	Decreasing, Export Controls	Strategy emerging to keep Taiwan at leading edge and off-shore trailing edge and associated value chain steps to mainland China.
China	Foundry, PV, LED	Design, Fabrication, Packaging, Testing	Constrained By Export Controls	Positive Growth in Trailing Edge ⬆	Very Involved, and Governments at National, State, and Local levels have equity stake in domestic firms.	Chinese government interested in developing capability to address new markets such as PV and LED.

Figure 3.22: Summary of East Asia Semiconductor Industry, 2010

Japan

Japan is still a major competitor in the chip industry, but its domestic economic turmoil and its inability to adapt to the changing semiconductor market have affected its standing.[84] Japan's older established chip firms are pursuing consolidation and are outsourcing design and fabrication outside of Japan.[85] Referencing the semiconductor value chain, Japanese semiconductor-equipment manufacturers (machines that fabricate the chips) are competitive and increasing shipments to China and Taiwan.[86] Japan is home to Nikon and Canon, the number two and number three firms of the top lithography companies in the world.[87] Japanese-headquartered companies are the world leaders in the packaging materials segment of the semiconductor industry, with a 2009 combined market share of 65 percent of an estimated $15.8 billion packaging-materials market.[88] Beyond encouraging energy-saving semiconductor applications, the Japanese government is not playing a major role in their mature domestic semiconductor industry.[89]

Korea

Korea's Samsung is the world leader in memory production and flat-panel displays, but the government is concerned about the concentration of its semiconductor industry in the memory market, continuing dependency on the import of integrated circuits for incorporation into consumer electronics, a slow start in creating a fabless sector, and the rise of China's industrial capability.[90] The Korean news media provides a sociocultural insight into perceptions of China's rise, characterizing Korean workers as avoiding the arduous work in semiconductor and LCD production, while their counterparts in China work at one-fifteenth of the annual salary of a Korean worker. That same article describes Korean firms as seeming to be horrified at the full-fledged efforts of high-ranking China officials to establish a predominant position in the semiconductor industry. The Korean semiconductor industry is concentrated in a few very large companies, of which Samsung is clearly the flagship. Korean-headquartered semiconductor packaging materials companies are increasing their overseas versus domestic sales, but in comparison to Japan, they remain a small player.[91] The remainder of Korea's firms on the semiconductor value chain primarily supply the domestic giants of electronics, LG and Samsung.[92] *EE Times* reports that the Korean government's "System IC 2010" project is an effort to jump-start the nation's fabless community, including analog

USING INDUSTRY ANALYSIS FOR STRATEGIC INTELLIGENCE

start-ups, but it is too early to see the results.[93] Samsung recognizes the risk of the company's concentration in memory and is expanding into the foundry arena, already scoring a significant win by producing the processor for Apple's new iPad.[94] Through its "low carbon, green growth" vision, the Korean government is supporting the industrialization of renewable energy sources as a driver for new employment and economic growth.[95]

Singapore

According to the Economic Development Board of Singapore, there are four 12-inch fabs in operation in Singapore by the world's top three wafer-foundry companies.[96] This island nation is also home to headquarters activities of over 125 electronic companies (including the 50 largest). Recently, U.S.-based Applied Materials opened its first facility in Asia for manufacturing its advanced semiconductor-fabrication equipment, citing that over 70 percent of its business is now in Asia.[97] Singapore's Chartered foundry (once 62 percent owned by the Singapore government's investment agency, Temasek Holdings) struggled to compete with Taiwan foundry's Taiwan Semiconductor Manufacturing Company (TSMC) and United Microelectronics Corporation (UMC), and was acquired in 2009 by the Advanced Technology Investment Company (ATIC), a wholly owned subsidiary of the Abu Dhabi government.[98] This acquisition, folded into the ATIC and AMD Global Foundries venture, creates a first-tier foundry competitor.

Taiwan

Taiwan is home to the world's two largest pure-play chip foundries—Taiwan Semiconductor Manufacturing Company (TSMC) and United Microelectronics Corporation (UMC)—and also has the largest number of LED fabs. Figure 3.23 shows that, in terms of integrated-circuit foundry sales, these two firms are positioned well ahead of their peer competitors.

2009 Major IC Foundries								
2009 Rank	Company	Foundry Type	Location	2007 Sales ($M)	2008 Sales ($M)	08/07 Sales %	2009 Sales ($M)	09/08 Sales %
1	TSMC	Pure-Play	Taiwan	9,813	10,556	8%	8,989	-15%
2	UMC	Pure-Play	Taiwan	3,430	3,070	-10%	2,815	-8%

2009 Major IC Foundries continued								
2009 Rank	Company	Foundry Type	Location	2007 Sales ($M)	2008 Sales ($M)	08/07 Sales %	2009 Sales ($M)	09/08 Sales %
3	Chartered*	Pure-Play	U.S.	1,458	1,743	20%	1,540	-12%
4	GlobalFoundries	Pure-Play	U.S.	0	0	N/A	1,101	N/A
5	SMIC	Pure-Play	China	1,550	1,353	-13%	1,075	-21%
6	Dongbu	Pure-Play	South Korea	510	490	-4%	395	-19%
7	Vanguard	Pure-Play	Taiwan	486	511	5%	382	-25%
8	IBM	IDM	U.S.	570	400	-30%	335	-16%
9	Samsung	IDM	South Korea	355	370	4%	325	-12%
10	Grace	Pure-Play	China	310	335	8%	310	-7%
11	He Jian	Pure-Play	China	330	345	5%	305	-12%
12	Tower**	Pure-Play	Europe	231	252	9%	292	16%
13	HHNEC	Pure-Play	China	335	350	4%	290	-17%
14	SSMC	Pure-Play	Singapore	350	340	-3%	280	-18%
15	TI	IDM	U.S.	450	315	-30%	250	-21%
16	X-Fab	Pure-Play	Europe	410	368	-10%	223	-39%
17	MagnaChip	IDM	South Korea	322	290	-10%	220	-24%

Source: IC Insights, company reports
*Purchased by GlobalFoundries in 4Q09.
**Tower bought Jazz in 2008.

Figure 3.23: TSMC Top among Foundries (© IC Insights, Company Reports)[99]

Given our previous discussion of the modularization of the semiconductor value chain and the rise of East Asia, it is not surprising to see the preponderance of foundries located there. The foundry model promises to shield a semiconductor firm from the intense capital costs of fabrication. It remains to be seen how far the fabless or fab-lite model will continue to progress.

Despite its history as the first chipmaker in Taiwan, UMC is seen as now falling behind the technology curve, succumbing to the continuing demands for capital to stay at the leading edge.[100] TSMC continues to grow, and expansion plans garner most of the news regarding Taiwan's semiconductor industry. At the front end of the value chain, TSMC's Electronic Design Automation plans and offerings have led some analysts to identify TSMC as a new integrated device manufacturer (IDM).[101] Also at the front end, TSMC announced its collaboration with MAPPER Lithography (a Netherlands firm) to incorporate a maskless lithography technology in its manufacturing processes.[102]

Akira Minamika, a speaker at SEMICON Japan, presented a slide (Figure 3.24) that reinforces the view that TSMC is going to grow beyond the business model of a pure-play foundry. TSMC's announcement that it is going to open an R&D center and wafer fab to develop and produce LEDs clearly establishes an IDM role for TSMC, as least in optoelectronics, despite its assurances that it will remain a pure-play foundry in the IC market sector.[103] This is significant, because a key selling point of a pure-play foundry is that it does not compete with its customers by producing its own line of chips.

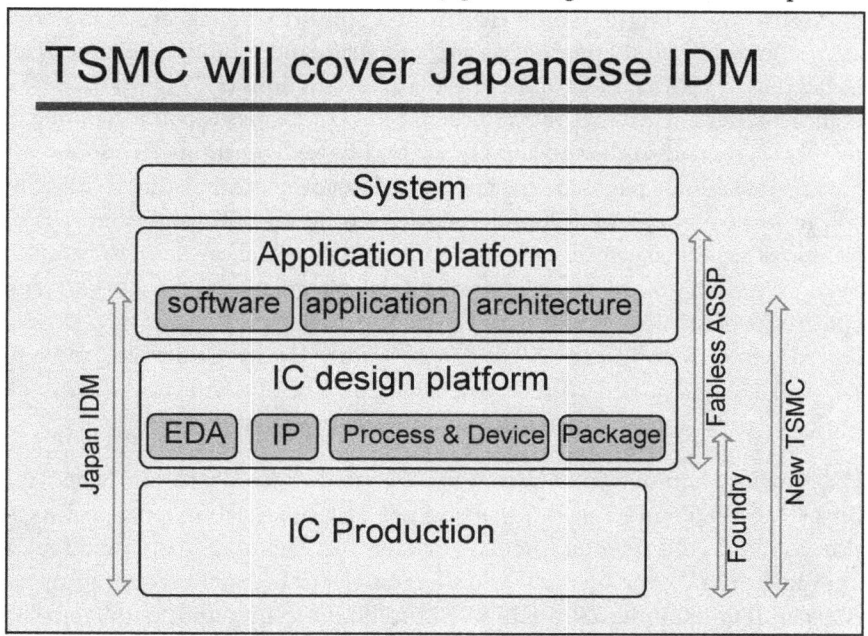

Figure 3.24: TSMC's Expanding Coverage (© IC Insights, Company Reports)[104]

Figure 3.24, provided at an industry tradeshow in Japan, highlights the recognition that TSMC is expanding its coverage of the value chain. This will be an interesting development, since Japanese firms use the foundry capabilities of TSMC and have not viewed TSMC as a competitor.

Although TSMC has a Samsung-like impact in its global stature, Taiwan has a more diverse semiconductor industry, with close ties to domestic and international electronics-manufacturing companies. Reflecting this strength of diversity is a recent legislative resolution that asks the Economics Ministry to discard a restructuring plan for Taiwan's DRAM industry, characterizing it as a waste of resources.[105] However, in the same session, it agreed to cut Taiwan's corporate tax rate from "20 to 17 percent and retain tax breaks targeted at R&D," which will sustain its national competitiveness.[106]

Strategic Intelligence Insight

The most interesting developments from a strategic intelligence perspective are the growing ties between Taiwan's and mainland China's semiconductor industries. In February 2010, Taiwan relaxed restrictions on "high-tech investment in China in another move to help local companies expand their global market shares and competitiveness."[107] The Taiwan Ministry of Economic Affairs will establish a panel to screen proposed investments. Existing regulations still in force prohibit local foundries from setting up 300 mm wafer fabs or foundries capable of processes below 130 nm, but will allow them to invest in or acquire China-based wafer foundries. Taiwan regulations now allow its chip companies to set up a maximum of three wafer fabs in China using processes less advanced than 0.18 micrometers (180 nm). The new rules also apply to low-end IC design and chip set packaging and testing industries, although projects greater than $50 million require screening for approval.[108]

Prior to this announcement, Taiwan's electronic manufacturing firms (the buyers of semiconductor chips) made use of China's labor force and location to build consumer end items. For example, Flextronics International, a Taiwan firm and one of the world's largest electronic manufacturing firms, is expanding its presence in China with a design center and manufacturing facilities in Wuzhong Export Processing Zone. This expansion complements its two existing computing design centers in Shanghai and Wujiang.[109] A government official in Taiwan allowed that the provisions on investments or

USING INDUSTRY ANALYSIS FOR STRATEGIC INTELLIGENCE

acquisitions of Chinese wafer foundries were meant to cover UMC's then-illegal investment in the Chinese foundry firm He Jian in 2006 and TSMC's pending stake in the Chinese foundry SMIC (a result of its successful intellectual property rights dispute with SMIC [Semiconductor Manufacturing International Corporation]).[110] Upon approval, UMC will be able to acquire the remaining 85 percent of He Jian, and TSMC will take a 10 percent stake in SMIC.[111] TSMC's chairman said they have no intent to take any day-to-day role in SMIC, and that they intend to keep their leading-edge fabs in Taiwan in order to take advantage of economies of scale; however, he also said they have submitted a technology-transfer application to produce higher-end circuits on its Shanghai wafer plant (about 200 mm fab).[112]

Smaller companies representing semiconductor value-chain activities are also strengthening ties to mainland firms. Chipbond Technology, a Taiwan firm that provides backend assembly processing for LCD driver ICs (a key component in LCD TVs), is requesting permission from the Taiwan government to increase its current holdings (20 percent) and take a majority share in China-based Chipmore Technology, in order to gain a foothold in China and its growing consumer market.[113] Taiwan's automotive industry, a consumer of ICs, is actively working to establish cross-strait agreements with China's automotive industry. Examples of IC applications include low-cost night vision systems, 360-degree viewing systems, and rain sensors.[114] A final, more conventional indicator of the increasing economic links between the two industries is illustrated by Taiwan's export statistics for May 2010: "[E]lectronics had the largest export value of $6.627B, rising by 47% on year and China (including Hong Kong) represents 43.8% of Taiwan's total export value."[115]

China

China's rise as an economic power is clear, but a subject of continuing debate is China's "openness" to reforms in governance and economics as it continues to develop. A single industry analysis can provide a degree of insight by the nature of its method of inquiry. Using our example of the semiconductor industry, here is the checklist of reasons why strategic insights on China are discoverable:

- The semiconductor industry is a priority for China.
- The technology and manufacturing leadership is centered in companies headquartered outside of China.

- The semiconductor industry has a history of openness in technology roadmaps and achievements.

- Semiconductor companies will not share their intellectual property or relocate manufacturing without openness in how their intellectual property is protected.

These points will be addressed as our analysis of results continues.

Figure 3.25 provides a map of the distribution and types of wafer fabs and foundries in China at the end of 2009.

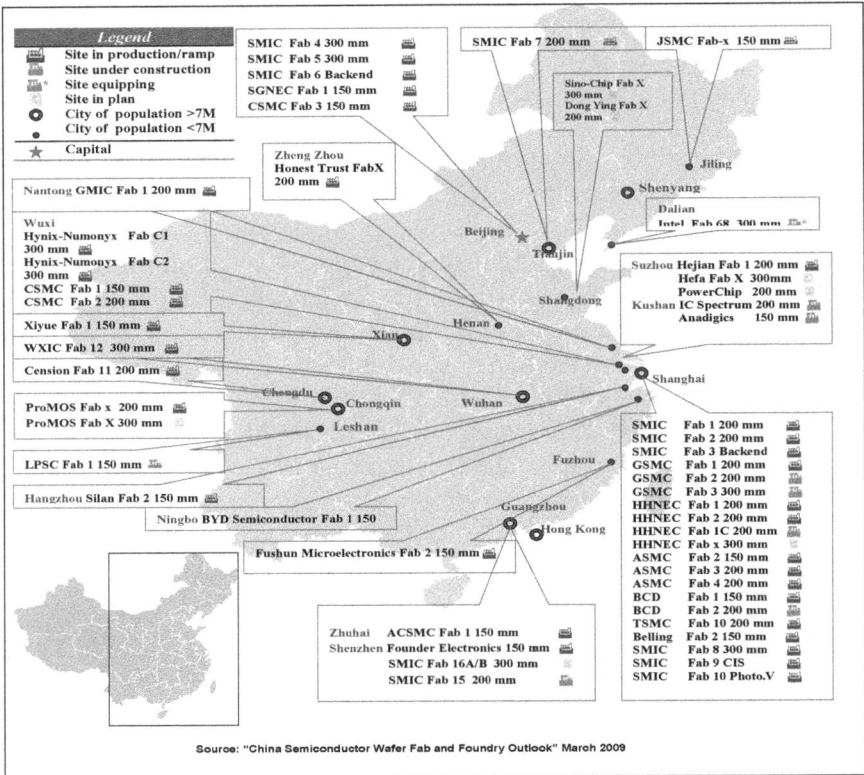

Figure 3.25: China Semiconductor Wafer Fab and Foundry Outlook (© SEMI)[116]

USING INDUSTRY ANALYSIS FOR STRATEGIC INTELLIGENCE

Studying the distribution and wafer-handling size of the semiconductor plants in China reveals several things. First, the majority of their capability cannot process 300 mm wafers, the current state of the art in the industry. Second, the majority of their manufacturing capability is clustered along the coastal areas. One factor driving this is the requirement to have a reliable infrastructure in place to support a semiconductor fab. This infrastructure must include reliable power, water, roads, and suppliers to support the 24/7 demands of a semiconductor fab.

China's government has a great interest in developing indigenous semiconductor fabrication capabilities. SEMI analysis of China includes the following excerpts:

> Since China surpassed Japan and the US in 2007 to become the world's largest consumer of ICs, China policy makers have increasingly voiced concerns about the 'chip gap' between supply and demand. In 2008, China consumed approximately one-quarter of the world's ICs, yet manufactured only $5.6 billion in chips, enough to support only 8% of their domestic requirements. By 2011, the China IC market will grow to $85 billion with domestic production expected to reach $8.2 billion, about 10% (iSupply, IC Insights, CSIA). By 2013, China's share of the global chip market will reach 35%. In the past, in markets such as computers, mobile phones, and automobiles, such an imbalance between supply and demand has prompted increased investments in local production capacity. ... [T]he Chinese government also remains the biggest investor in the semiconductor industry in China. In the past five years, the China government influenced the investment of about $7 billion in new fabs. In the next five years, local government will likely continue to be the significant co-investor in strategic IC Fab projects throughout the country. Going forward, the central government may also invest up to $30 billion on semiconductor (semiconductor equipment and material are included), also software and high-end chip hardware industry by 2020.[117]

The profitability of China's leading-edge foundry, SMIC, provides insights into the government's progress. In 2000, the governments of Beijing, Shanghai, Wuhan, Chengdu, and Guangzhou put forward the resources to support SMIC.[118] After 10 years of investment, as Figure 3.26 illustrates, SMIC, China's bid to create a leading-edge foundry, has yet to turn a profit.[119]

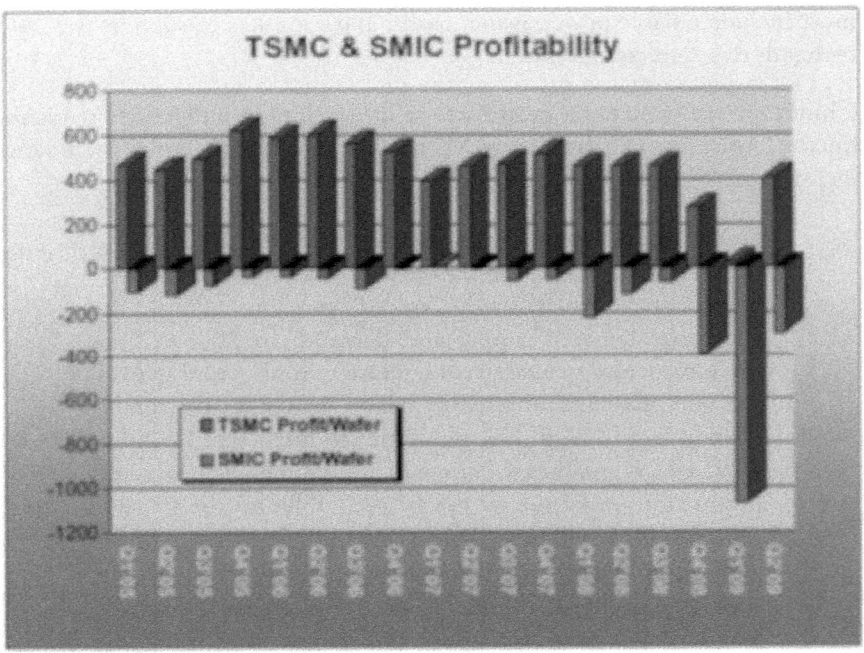

Figure 3.26: Profitability of Taiwan and Mainland China's Leading-Edge Foundries (© VLSIresearch. In "China Leads World Out of Recession, Through Recovery." January 14, 2010, *Semiconductor International*.)[120]

Figure 3.26 shows that, on a profit-per-wafer basis, Taiwan's TSMC has clearly outperformed China's SMIC. In addition to infrastructure requirements, a semiconductor fab has equally demanding process requirements. A high degree of process maturity is required in order to achieve success (both in terms of quality of product and turning a profit) in operating a semiconductor fab. SMIC's profit performance and TSMC's out-of-court settlement with SMIC (due to SMIC's theft of intellectual property belonging to TSMC) led to a turnover in SMIC leadership.[121] All of this indicates

USING INDUSTRY ANALYSIS FOR STRATEGIC INTELLIGENCE

that China's semiconductor industry has not attained the required process maturity required for leading-edge IC fabrication.

Recognizing that the bulk of the semiconductor market is in the trailing edge, taking advantage of the economic downturn, and the migration of the industry to 300 mm equipment, the trade press believes that China will invest billions over the next several years into repurposing and refurbishing 200 mm and 300 mm fabs, and utilizing primarily used and refurbished equipment.[122] Referencing some of the earlier figures showing the relative rankings of semiconductor firms, it is clear that the largest companies still reside outside of China. Also, the research and development expenditures of these industry leaders are much greater than China has been willing or able to invest.

China's intellectual-property laws and their enforcement are still a work in progress. One company characterizes patent enforcement in China as "slightly improved from terrible to bad," and said that China now concentrates enforcement on discovering export items to Europe, Japan, and the United States that illegally use China's intellectual property, recognizing that enforcement within China is not possible.[123] One rationale for TSMC's out-of-court settlement with SMIC is that it did not want to bankrupt SMIC and risk TSMC's intellectual property being acquired or lost entirely.[124] Now, TSMC, with its minority share, can closely monitor SMIC's use of TSMC's technology. The IBM Corporation is very adept at handling intellectual-property licensure for semiconductor processes, only raising eyebrows in the industry by offering technology that may allow Chinese firms to "catch up."[125]

Freescale, a U.S. semiconductor design firm, has five IC design centers in China, and describes its Chengdu center as "the front lines in the development and customization in the networking-chip arena."[126] One approach to protecting intellectual property would appear to be in jointly developing technology with China. Intel Capital, the Intel Corporation's global investment arm, and China Investment Corporation (CIC) announced that they are going to pair CIC's resources with Intel Capital's technology expertise to make strategic investments in pioneering for companies engaged in the next generation of groundbreaking technologies.[127] Although the agreement states that the investments will be outside of China, this is an interesting development to watch in order to understand the extent of the globalization of intellectual property.

As related earlier, many of the largest firms in the industry locate only less important processing or fabrication steps in China, sometimes due to export control laws, but also due to concerns about intellectual-property infringement. For example, Intel continues to run its leading-edge fabs outside of China in order to protect its microprocessor and process technology. Applied Materials operations in China has taken measures to prevent intellectual-property theft, such as "sealing its computers' ports in Xian, to prevent easy use of flash drives"; controlling removal of computers by employees; and maintaining computer passwords and door codes to control technology access.[128] Applied Materials continues to conduct its research and development in laboratories in the United States and Europe, but put its first Asian equipment-manufacturing operation in Singapore, where protection of intellectual property is more developed. Despite the risks of intellectual-property theft, the rising purchasing power of China's population, and governmental trade and tax policies, the semiconductor industry is placing more capability in China.

The example of Applied Materials and the establishment of a laboratory for assembly-line design in Xian illustrate the financial incentives for establishing operations in China. According to an article in the *International Herald Tribune*, first the Xian city government sold a 75-year land lease to Applied Materials at a deep discount, and then it reimbursed the company for about a quarter of the complex's operating costs for five years.[129] Thomas J. Friedman, an op-ed columnist with *The New York Times*, interviewed Paul Otellini, the CEO of Intel, comparing the incentives in the United States with those in China:

> "The things that are not conducive to investments here are [corporate] taxes and capital equipment credits," he said. "A new semiconductor factory at world scale built from scratch is about $4.5 billion—in the United States. If I build that factory in almost any other country in the world, where they have significant incentive programs, I could save $1 billion," because of all the tax breaks these governments throw in. Not surprisingly, the last factory Intel built from scratch was in China. "That comes online in October [2010]," he said. "And it wasn't because the labor costs are lower. Yeah, the construction costs were a little bit lower, but the cost of operating when you look at it after tax was substantially lower and you have local market access."[130]

USING INDUSTRY ANALYSIS FOR STRATEGIC INTELLIGENCE

Incentives to relocate to China are available to many countries, but they are not always financial incentives. An article in *Business Week* stated that Yukio Sakamoto, the president of Elpida Memory Inc., Japan's sole maker of computer-memory chips, announced plans to build factories in Taiwan and China to meet demand and reduce tax payments. Reading further in the article, it is clear Elpida is also relocating to avoid Chinese import tariffs.[131] In the same article, Intel (United States) and Hynix (Korea) set up factories in China "to avoid a 17 percent value-added tax that applies to chips imported into China and used in electronics sold domestically."

Despite China's outwardly successful mix of incentives and tax policies, the original equipment manufacturers (OEMs), assemblers of final end items for consumption, are still very cost conscious and will move to lower-cost areas of the world if it is more profitable. China's rising labor costs, increases in energy prices, quality problems, intellectual-property theft, and a global modular value chain keep other regions of the world as viable alternatives.[132]

When the economic downturn occurred in 2009, many Chinese workers left the coastal area and returned home to inland areas. Now, with the economic recovery and China's stimulus spending, many of these workers find work at home and are not migrating back to the coastal areas—inflating wages in the coastal areas, where electronics manufacturing is centered.[133]

On the environmental-regulatory front, China is planning to implement REACH (Register, Evaluation, and Authorization of Chemicals) regulations similar to the European Union's REACH. The REACH regulations require companies to declare the types and uses of chemicals in production and also include chemicals released during the end products' normal use.[134] The effects and enforcement of these regulations on the semiconductor industry remain to be seen.

China is aggressively pursuing all the new avenues of profitability. As shown earlier, China has a large number of LED fabs in operation. In photovoltaic (PV) production, already noted is Applied Materials' opening of the world's largest solar research center in China. Domestically, China's government is working with their PV Industry Association to assist in setting up a photovoltaic industry alliance for research and standards setting. It might be a strategic insight to say that, in order for China to incorporate the PV industry into its energy economy, it will need to set standards for PV components and grid connections, improve those grid connections, and resolve the economics of getting PV-generated power (requiring large open areas) to distant population areas.[135] Figure 3.27 illustrates the PV cluster areas in China.

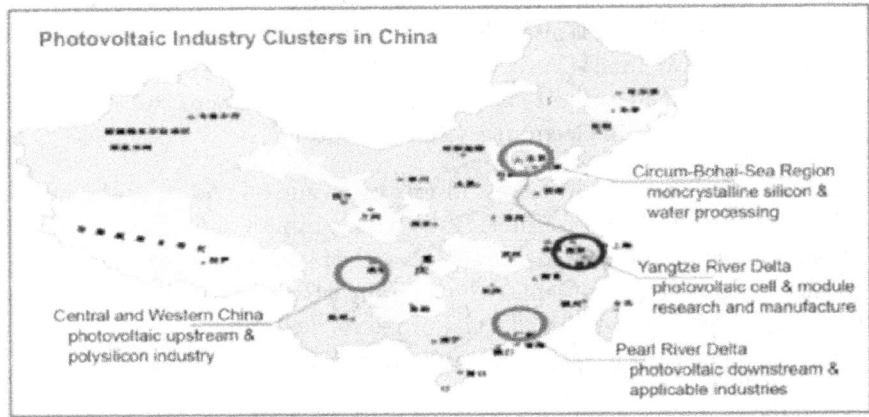

Figure 3.27: China's Photovoltaic Industry (© ResearchinChina)[136]

While Figure 3.27 provides the location of industry clusters for mainland China PV manufacturers, more important is the previous citation that describes the Chinese government's hosting of meetings to set standards and share information among the domestic PV companies.

Medical-device applications provide a sociocultural view into China and why the semiconductor industry is looking at China as a large potential market. An article in *EE Times China* states:

> The portable/home electro-medical device market is enjoying a fast and stable expansion in China due to the government's medical reform, citizens' concern in healthcare, and the unique features the devices are offering.
>
> The CAGR of portable electro-medical device market is expected to go up significantly, with market survey showing rapid expansion from 8 billion yuan ($1.17 billion) in 2006 to 28 billion yuan ($4.1 billion) in 2011. "The market is proven to have a powerful anti-risk capability because the whole

market is oriented toward China's internal demand and is basically insusceptible to the global financial crises. In China, the market is only in the initial startup phase, so the market demand is huge. In addition, the Chinese have an increasingly high consciousness of health," Zhou Wensheng, senior sales manager of ADI's medical division in Asia-Pacific, said.

Like ADI, the worldwide semiconductor manufacturers cast more eyes on the portable/home electro-medical device market of China. Looking forward to the future, everyone will have multiple portable medical devices rather than just one, making it a more exciting market than the cell phones. After losing the country's huge mobile phone market, numerous Europe and U.S. companies are expected to try their best to get a share of the portable/home electro-medical device market of China. "China and the world have a huge demand for the portable electro-medical devices, and China will enter the list of the largest electro-medical device manufacturers and largest markets," Fan Xujin, chief product marketing engineer of Microchip's medical product division, said.[137]

Summary

While Japan was the leading challenger to the U.S. lead in the semiconductor industry in the 1980s, Japan's domestic economic challenges have slowed the growth of its semiconductor industry. Important is the decline of Japanese firms in manufacturing lithography equipment (the basis for the key value-chain activity, mask creation). Japanese companies Nikon and Canon were the leaders in the lithography-equipment market, but they are now overshadowed by the market leader ASML, headquartered in the Netherlands. If business conditions do not change, ASML will have a virtual monopoly on leading-edge lithography equipment.

The Korean firm Samsung is the world's leader in semiconductor memory, but its enormous size has not translated into development of a broader semiconductor industry in Korea.

Singapore is the leader in hosting the regional headquarters functions of almost all the major semiconductor companies in the world. But Singapore's divestment of Chartered Semiconductor to outside investors leaves open the question of its future industrial capability.

Taiwan is a success story in joint government and private industry development of an industrial base capability. Taiwan's semiconductor industry is conscious of the challenges of staying at the leading edge and is pursuing cost savings by off-shoring trailing-edge and associated value-chain steps to lower-cost areas, such as mainland China.

Mainland China has a strategy to develop an indigenous capability to supply the chips that they currently must import for both domestic and export industries. Various levels of government in China provide incentives and equity backing to domestic semiconductor firms. After a decade of investing to establish a leading-edge foundry in China, the government is now content to buy up trailing-edge semiconductor fabrication equipment and relocate it to China. In the PV- and LED-fabrication sectors, where there are no leading-edge export controls, China is rapidly building up value-chain elements tailored to these market sectors. Analyzing the semiconductor industry and East Asia provides some strategic insights.

Despite China's juggernaut appearance in technology advancement, the leading edge of semiconductors represents a difficult level to attain and, as a result, China is slowing its indigenous leading-edge development. China's internal market potential, incentives, and tax policies are attracting the placement of semiconductor operations in China, but concerns about intellectual property are still valid. As the foremost consideration, if higher profits can be earned in manufacturing outside of China, then manufacturers will relocate elsewhere, despite China's policies. A sign of China's rising consumer population is forecasted to increase demand for cell phones, LCD TVs, and medical devices within China.

A strategic insight that rises up to the level of strategic intelligence insights is the growing economic ties between mainland China and Taiwan. Taiwan industries are leveraging Chinese industry in pursuit of competitive advantage. China is gaining advanced technology and building its industries through ties to Taiwan and other nations. This insight will be developed and discussed further in the next chapter's concluding discussion and evaluation of the value of industry analysis to the Intelligence Community.

Chapter Four

Conclusion

An all-source intelligence analyst can use the analysis tools of business strategists and competitive intelligence professionals in analyzing an industry in another country or region of the world. By using these tools, an analyst is able to develop strategic intelligence insights about a nation's plans and intentions. The main conclusions to be drawn are as follows: (1) industry analysis is easy to grasp and only a little harder to apply; (2) the results of industry analysis provide a useful lens for intelligence-collection analysis and synthesis; and (3) globalization has become a defining force in the world, and merits more attention from the Intelligence Community.

Applying Industry Analysis

The application of industry analysis is, first and foremost, not a major break with the conduct of all-source analysis. Industry analysis will provide a lens (or frame of reference) that complements the existing repertoire of analysis tools within the Intelligence Community. At a minimum, it offers a better alternative than performing a keyword search on open-source business and industry information.

Follow the Steps

The steps for conducting industry analysis are straightforward and meant to be easily internalized. The first steps of selecting and defining the industry for analysis will be the most difficult. For one thing, selecting an industry that will yield strategic insights automatically excludes countries that, while of interest to the Intelligence Community, do not have a developing industry sector or choose not to participate in the global economy. Second, defining an industry is time-consuming, but its practice (and, concurrently, the exposure to economics and industry structure) will serve the analyst in defining other industries in the future. Using the models described earlier will facilitate a focused review and selection of sources.

The collection and analysis steps are the most straightforward for the all-source analyst. At that point, the analyst will understand the nuances of the industry information before him or her and have a framework for collection and analysis. The major difference in these steps, between the business analyst and the all-source analyst, is the strategic perspective the all-source analyst brings to the task. In addition, the all-source analyst can synthesize the findings with other Intelligence Community inputs to improve strategic understanding.

Utility of Industry Analysis

In the last chapter, the major strategic-intelligence insight points to the growing economic ties between mainland China and Taiwan. Analysis of the semiconductor industry provides this insight, but also lays the foundation for future analysis of other industries, such as the automotive industry, to see if they are also fostering cross-strait ties.

Another topic for further exploration is mainland China's progress in rebuilding its power-generation infrastructure to handle alternative "green" power generation and applications. The photovoltaic and light-emitting diode industries (subsets of the semiconductor industry) provide a window into a challenge that the United States also faces. It is now clear that mainland China has an interest in developing its indigenous semiconductor industry and is willing to deal with Taiwan in pursuit of that goal. This strategic insight lasers through the unpredictability of nationalism or geopolitical flare-ups.

Utilizing the addition of a new lens for intelligence analysis is achievable at the level of the all-source analyst by examining current national intelligence estimates to see how our strategic insight above "fits" with the prevailing view within the Intelligence Community. The classification of national intelligence estimates leaves this action outside of this book. Ian Bremmer, however, in his book *The End of the Free Market*, offers an interesting strategic assessment independent of our industry analysis in the context of discussing the challenges posed by state-sponsored capitalism:

> Beijing's primary military concern is the risk of a direct or proxy conflict with the United States over Taiwan. But the Chinese leadership is well aware that no U.S. government will support a Taiwanese bid for independence, and why should the Chinese launch a self-defeating invasion of the

island when it can co-opt most of Taiwan's business elite with privileged access to investment opportunities on the mainland? So far, globalization has been good to China's Communist Party, and wars are bad for business.[138]

It is important to point out that the inclusion of industry analysis is meant to enhance the national-intelligence estimate, not drive startling new conclusions. What is suggested here is that too great a focus on political and military dimensions by the Intelligence Community leads to discounting the influence of economics in international politics.[139] The strategic-intelligence insights we seek come from examining the "contours" of industry interactions with foreign governments, and any contributions to a national-intelligence estimate resulting from these strategic-intelligence insights will be in the "contours" of the estimate. As a result, the final utility or value-added assessment of industry analysis remains within the analysis community.

Increased Attention by the Intelligence Community to Globalization

In the introductory chapter, the background question of the role of the Intelligence Community in assessing the effects of globalization came with a brief historical perspective. A couple of the points from this perspective are worth highlighting. First, the Intelligence Community at one time believed that the way a nation (the Soviet Union) acted in the economic sphere was likely to reveal its intentions. Second, policymakers' interest in the community's industry analysis was motivated by perceptions of the United States potentially being outperformed economically and militarily by the Soviet Union.

The Soviet Union is consigned to the history books, and there is no concern about a renaissance of centralized command economies among the world's nations. But there is a relatively new competitor to the U.S. free-market system, which is a "state-sponsored capitalism" that may spark an interest in reviving industry analysis within the Intelligence Community. State-sponsored capitalism "is a system in which the state dominates markets primarily for political gain."[140] The recent acquisition of Chartered Semiconductor in Singapore highlighted earlier is an example of state-sponsored capitalism at work. The Singapore government's holding company was a major shareholder in Chartered and approved its sale to a joint venture by a holding company of the Abu Dhabi government and the publicly traded semiconductor firm

AMD.[141] This exchange was in part a nation-to-nation business transaction that, in the case of Abu Dhabi, solely benefits the ruling family.

Ian Bremmer notes that state-sponsored capitalism is not protectionism for developing national competitiveness; it is the state "using markets to create wealth that can be directed as political officials see fit."[142] Put another way, the major difference in state-sponsored capitalism vis-à-vis free-market capitalism is that the overriding objective of state-sponsored capitalism is maintaining the party in power, not the prosperity of its people.[143]

The potential for the United States being outperformed economically and militarily is open for debate, but it should not be the threshold for reawakening industry analysis within the Intelligence Community. The global interdependencies between nations are a fact and, in the case of U.S.-China relations, have even earned the catchphrase "mutually assured economic destruction." This play on the Cold War term "'mutually assured destruction' is not to suggest that a new cold war is upon us, but that the battle for the free market is a battle for national competitiveness that must avoid catastrophic outcomes."[144] Even though the current priorities of the Intelligence Community reflect its customers' requirements, there is a need for the community to step up and enhance its intelligence offerings with insights into globalization and its potential effects on national security.

Appendixes

Appendix A

External Environment Model Segments and Elements[145]

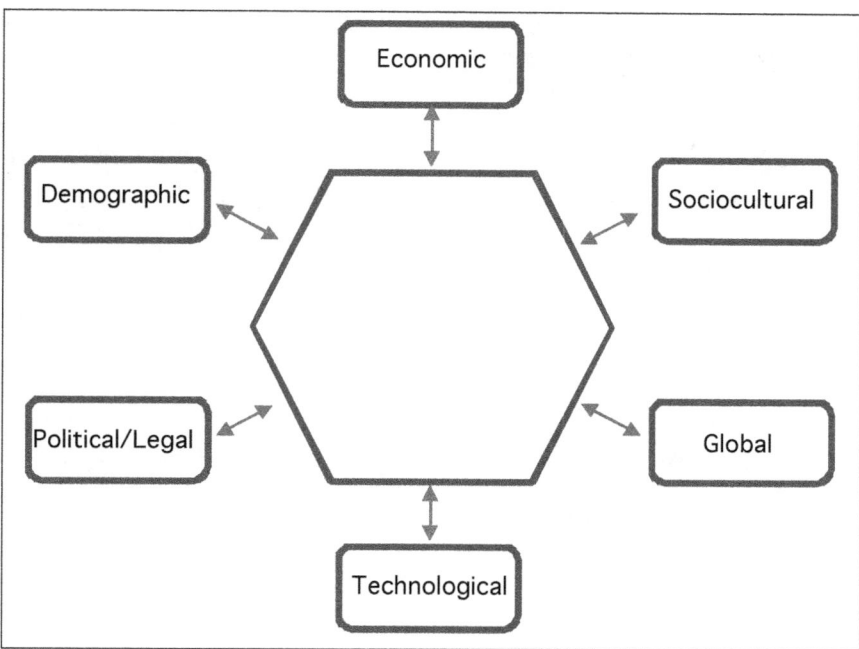

Source: Adapted from Hoskisson, Hitt, and Ireland.

Demographic

Population Size, Age/Gender Structure, Geographic Distribution, Ethnic Mix

Economic

Distribution/Uses of Resources, Impact of Global Economy on Domestic Economy/ Markets, Macroeconomic Factors

Sociocultural

Cultural Attitudes, Customs, Values, Education/Skill Levels, Workforce Diversity, Attitudes about Quality of Work Life, Concerns about Environment

Global

Important Political Events, New Markets, Changes to Existing Markets, Different Cultural and Institutional Attributes

Technological

Product Innovations, Focus of Private and Government-Supported R&D Expenditures, New Technologies

Political/Legal

Appendix B
Semiconductor Industry Tutorial

The purpose of this appendix is to provide a brief tutorial on semiconductors, the key activities involved in their development, and the size and composition of their market. Chapter 2 introduces three models to use in industry analysis, and Chapter 3 describes a methodology for selecting an industry for analysis, which, for the purposes of this book, is the semiconductor industry. The next step is to define the selected industry, which in this case requires developing a broad understanding of the semiconductor industry. This understanding will first be put to use in developing a value chain for the industry. The development of a value chain is an iterative process; it reflects and reinforces your understanding of the industry. It is quite possible that a value chain is already available from open sources. If so, it can be used as a guide for sorting out the key activities and processes involved in producing semiconductors. Following the industry definition step, the value chain will be put to further use during the collection and analysis of information on the semiconductor industry.

Since the technology behind semiconductors is over 60 years old, there is a wealth of open-source information on the semiconductor industry, both in print and on the Internet. What will become readily apparent is how far that technology has progressed, especially in process development and applications. There are useful glossaries of industry-related terms available on the Internet. This appendix will cite several for definitions so the analyst has a choice of sources in case a website becomes unavailable.[146] To understand an industry, a basic understanding of its products and markets is necessary. For the semiconductor industry, product knowledge equates to a basic understanding of semiconductors and their development into integrated circuits. Research into the size and composition of the semiconductor market brings into focus the globalization of the industry and its importance to developed and developing nations of the world.

Gain knowledge of semiconductors and their development into integrated circuits.

Devices made from semiconductor materials are the foundation of the computer and communications industries. Also familiar are the multitude of consumer-oriented electronic devices (such as cell phones) in use in almost every corner of the earth. Semiconductors are also increasingly used in the automotive and medical-devices industries, and form the basis for promising devices for saving or generating energy.[147] One surprising fact is that, although it was the U.S. federal government's funding of basic research and government demand for electronics that fueled the early growth of this industry, today the government constitutes less than 1 percent of the semiconductor market.[148]

The first question to answer is: what are semiconductors? A semiconductor is a material that has the properties of a conductor and an insulator. The exact properties are determined during the production of the silicon crystal and the processing of the wafer that provides the platform for the integrated circuit. The fabrication process described here is referred to as CMOS (complementary metal-oxide semiconductor) and is the industry's main manufacturing platform.[149] Figure B.1 illustrates the process for creating the silicon crystal.

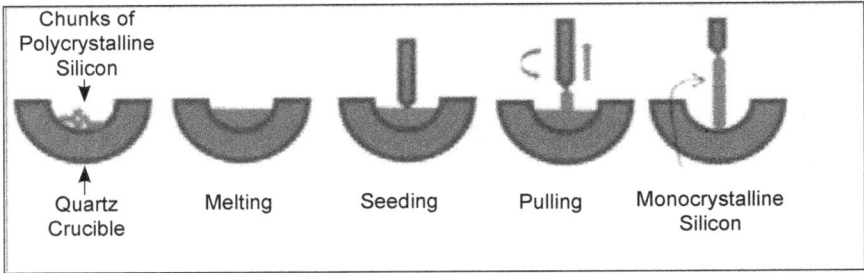

Figure B.1: Crystal Growth[150]

There are several methods for creating the silicon crystal for wafers. The process in Figure B.1 is common and the one most likely to be found in diagrams, pictures, or video on the semiconductor process. The rough silicon material is noteworthy because, while it is a common material, there can be temporary shortages of supply due to the cyclical nature of the semiconductor market. The raw material is melted in a furnace.[151] The next step, called *seeding*, involves lowering a single silicon crystal into the molten material. The molten silicon immediately affixes itself to the seed, forming a single crystal, and while the seed is slowly withdrawn, its simultaneous rotation produces the resulting cylindrical shape. The cylinder of pure silicon is often referred to as a boule.[152] The process is controlled to produce the desired diameter of the finished wafer. A wafer is defined as "a thin slice with parallel faces cut from a semiconductor crystal."[153] Wafers are produced in a wide variety of sizes and characteristics. The state of the practice now produces up to 300 mm (about 12 inches in diameter) wafers.

To create the wafers, the boule is removed from the furnace and the two ends are sawed off. Figure B.2 shows the entire boule cut into the thin slices referred to as the wafers. Following this, the wafers are run through a lapping process to remove surface irregularities and produce a uniform flat surface. Lapping involves placing the wafer on a revolving surface with a constant stream of a fine abrasive material, and then another surface revolving in the opposite direction placed above. The sandwiching of the wafer between the counter-rotating surfaces and the wet abrasive gradually removes irregularities. The etching step is a chemical process to remove any crystal damage from lapping. Polishing, the final step, smooths the uneven surface left by the lapping and etching and makes the wafer flat and smooth.

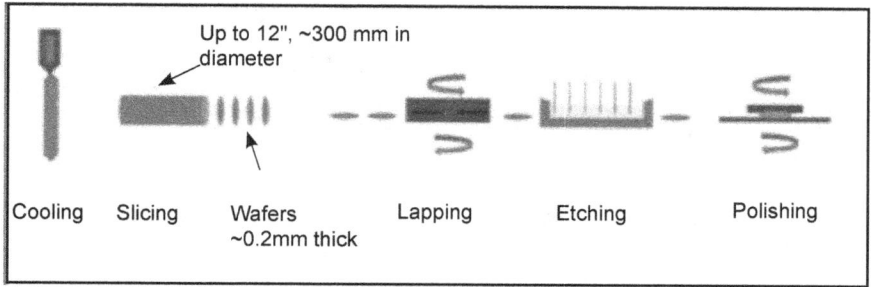

Figure B.2: Wafer Processing

Integrated Circuits

A wafer is composed of a semiconductor material and is the platform for the process that creates integrated circuits, which are then packaged into chips. An integrated circuit, or IC, is created on a wafer, usually made of silicon, and can hold anywhere from hundreds to hundreds of millions of electronic components, such as transistors, resistors, and capacitors.[154]

Transistor Density

The familiar phrase "Moore's Law" is frequently referred to in articles regarding the semiconductor industry. In reality, Moore's Law is not a law at all; it is an observation made by Gordon Moore in the 1960s and later revised in the 1970s. His observation, remarkably prescient, is that the transistor densities on integrated circuits will double every two years.[155] Transistor density is important because more transistors equates to more functions in a smaller space, lower power requirements, and, with economies of scale, lower cost. Figure B.3 provides an example of increasing capability and decreasing price for semiconductor memory.

Reduced Memory Cost Drives New Architecture and Applications

	1979	1984	2001	2005	2007
	SONY WALKMAN	SONY DISCMAN	IPOD ORIGINAL	IPOD NANO	IPOD TOUCH
Storage Technology	Cassette Tape	CD	Hard Drive	Flash	Flash
Storage Size	60 MB (20 songs)	700 MB (26 songs)	5 GB (1,000 songs)	4 GB (800 songs)	16 GB (3,200 songs)
Cost	$200	$299	$400	$249	$399
Device Cost per Song	$10	$11.50	$0.40	$0.31	$0.13

Figure B.3: Memory Example (© Mentor Graphics)[156]

All of these are what the industry and its customers have come to expect. Figure B.4 illustrates how Moore's Law is still a driving force in the semiconductor industry:

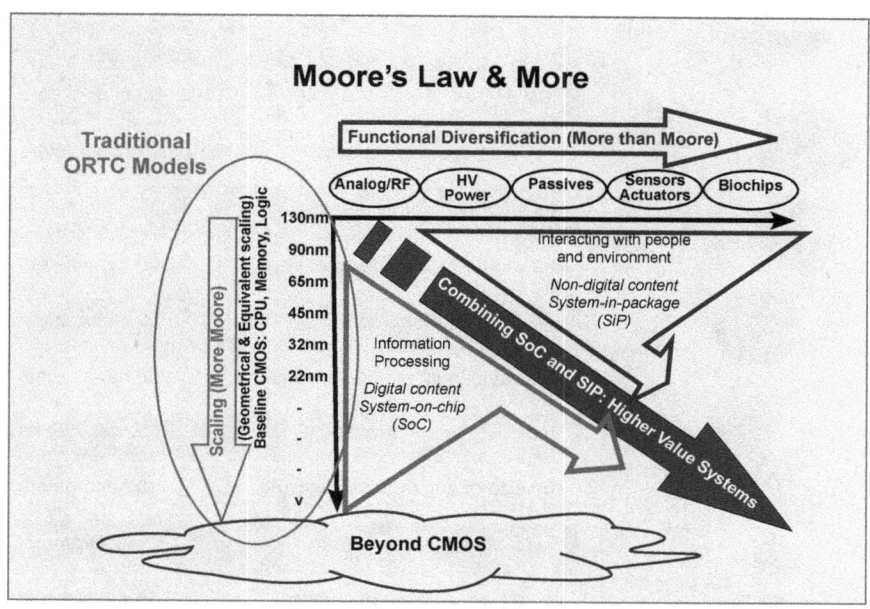

Figure B.4: Beyond Moore's Law (© Semiconductor Industry Association)[157]

Note that the y-axis scale shows decreasing numbers, with "nm"—nanometers, or a billionth of a meter—appended to each. The numbers refer to the width of the smallest feature—"feature size"—on an integrated circuit.

Feature Size

Almost all trade journal issues bring up the topic of feature size, typically by using the shorthand of providing the scale of the integrated circuits in nanometers. Figure B.5 provides a pictorial representation of the comparative size of objects on a nanometer scale.

How many nanometers is …	Approximately
The width of a hair	100,000 nanometers
The width of a red blood cell	10,000 nanometers
The length of a typical bacterium	1,000 nanometers
The width of a dust particle	800 nanometers
The wavelength of red light	650 nanometers
The wavelength of ultraviolet light	300 nanometers
The length of a typical virus	100 nanometers
The size of a membrane enzyme	10 nanometers
The width of a carbon atom	1 nanometer
The distance between carbon atoms	0.15 nanometers

Figure B.5: Size Comparison (© Northwestern University Nanoscale Science and Engineering Center); Images in Nanoscale (© Dennis Kunkel Microscopy, Inc.); Table by Waldron and Batt (© McNeil-Lehrer Productions)[158]

Referring to Figure B.5, feature sizes below 25 nm are now going into production. This means the size of an individual circuit path on a chip is smaller than the length of a virus and a little larger than a strand of DNA. A topic of much discussion is: what comes after the limits of scaling are reached?

Chip Design

The process for creating chips starts with the design. The software used in designing chips is an entire industry unto itself. It is called the electronic design automation (EDA) industry, and this industry develops and sustains integrated circuit design tools. EDA Consortium, the electronic design automation industry trade association, also has a web-accessible video that quickly describes the entire semiconductor design and fabrication process.[159] The design for

USING INDUSTRY ANALYSIS FOR STRATEGIC INTELLIGENCE

an integrated circuit is captured on digital files that are used throughout the manufacturing process.[160] These digital files are representative of the information exchange that characterizes a modularized value chain.

Chip Fabrication

Figure B.6 provides a simplified view of this process. The design information is first used to create a mask. In simple terms, the mask is a clear piece of quartz, referred to as a reticle, which is etched with one level of the integrated circuits' design. Today's integrated circuits may have many layers, so there would be a reticle for each layer. Using lithography, a process similar to processing photographs, the wafer is coated in a material referred to as "photoresist"; then a light is projected through the reticle, and that layer of the design is transferred via exposure to the wafer. A key step in process planning is maximizing the number of copies of the design layer that can be placed on the wafer. Each of those copies on the wafer is referred to as a "die." Per the design files, the wafer is then sent off to additional processing; one step removes the exposed photoresist, leaving the design of the integrated circuit behind. The wafer is then recoated with photoresist and is exposed using the reticle containing the next level of the design.

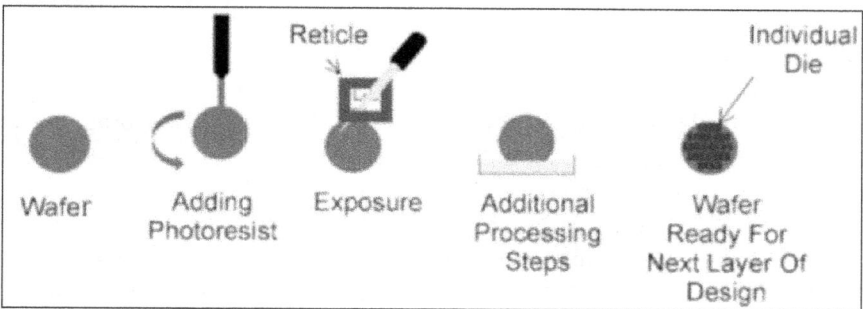

Figure B.6: Fabrication Steps

Referring to Figure B.6, the bare wafer on the left is ready to start the fabrication process. The wafer is coated with photoresist and then moved to the lithography station, where it is exposed to light. The reticle (also referred to as the mask) is a thin piece of quartz that is etched with one level of the integrated circuits' design. The mask holds a layer of the design and, when the wafer coated with photoresist is exposed to a light source, the areas of the wafer not obscured by the design pattern on the mask are exposed. This wafer is then put through a series of chemical baths that strip away the exposed photoresist on the wafer, leaving the layer of the design untouched. The wafer is then re-covered with photoresist and run through the lithography station, and then put through a series of chemical baths to strip away the photoresist and leave the second layer of the design on the wafer.

To process the wafer with multiple mask sets (one mask for each layer on the individual chip) takes weeks. Since the processing steps for a typical forty-layer chip design take so long, and it is cost-prohibitive to build an additional line, semiconductor companies pursue other options, such as increasing the number of chips they produce on each pass through the process.

One approach for increasing the number of chips produced is to increase the wafer size. The industry standard is currently a 300 mm wafer (roughly 12 inches in diameter). The industry movement from 200 mm to 300 mm wafers provided an increase of 125 percent in surface area on which to produce integrated circuits (dies). For example, this transition means that for a die size of 161.3 square millimeters (approximately ¼ square inches), the fabrication line is processing 376 dies per wafer on a 300 mm wafer versus 148 dies on a 200 mm wafer.[161]

The industries' nine-year transition from 200 mm to 300 mm and the cost of developing an entirely new process line are not lost on the equipment manufacturers. While 300 mm wafer processing continues to deliver productivity improvements, that transition did not translate into higher profit margins for the semiconductor-equipment industry. The industry is currently debating a move to a 450 mm wafer (a 125 percent increase over 300 mm), but only a few of the industry leaders are showing interest, and there is no agreed-to business model that shows funding for the transition and also provides a reasonable return on investment for the semiconductor-equipment manufacturers.[162]

Chip Packaging

Figure B.7 shows the continuation of the fabrication process once all of the integrated circuit design is on the wafer. When all of the design is processed into the wafer, each die on the wafer is tested, and any defective dies are marked. The individual dies are then cut from the wafer and undergo further testing.

USING INDUSTRY ANALYSIS FOR STRATEGIC INTELLIGENCE

The usable dies are attached to frames and, after wire bonding and encapsulation, they are chips ready for placement in their intended application.

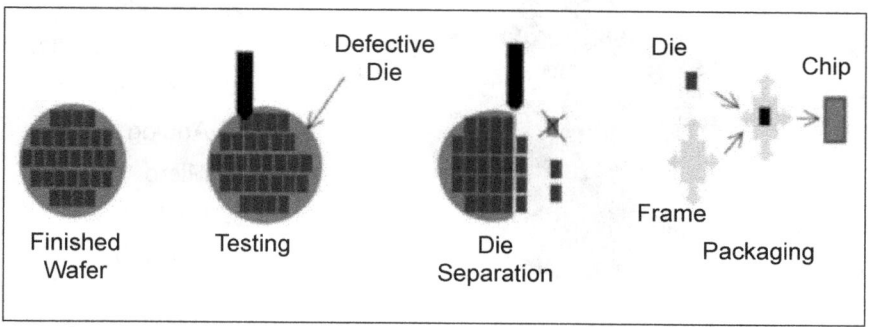

Figure B.7: Die Testing and Packaging

The semiconductor industry is technology driven and requires a continuing investment in research and development to produce the advances observed by Moore's Law. Equipment to produce a leading-edge computer chip costs hundreds of millions of dollars.[163] A basic understanding of the fabrication of semiconductors is possible in a short amount of time. The fact that global industry is trying to figure out how to reduce feature size so it can deliver increased performance in ever-smaller packages is readily apparent without requiring a technical degree or know-how.

Understand the size and composition of the semiconductor market.

Industry trade associations, industry trade press, international trade organizations, market research firms, and government documents are just a few of the available sources for market information. For the semiconductor industry, the World Semiconductor Trade Statistics, a nonprofit corporation, compiles industry trade statistics and provides market forecasts.[164] The data is provided by the member semiconductor companies and is considered to be a reliable source of information. The top-level forecasts are provided free via their website. For 2008, the world semiconductor market was $248.6 billion, and Figure B.8 shows the major market segments and their relative percentage of the total market.

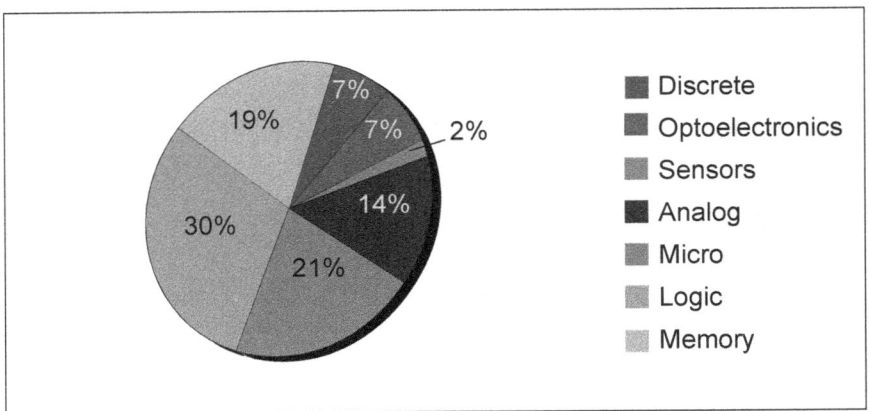

Figure B.8: Total World Semiconductor Market, 2008—$248.6 Billion[165]

A look at the composition of the semiconductor market segments reveals that logic, memory, and micro devices are the largest segments. The IC Insights glossary cited earlier and the Semiconductor Glossary provide the following definitions for the semiconductor market segments shown in the figure:[166]

- **Discrete**—A class of electronic components that includes power transistors and rectifiers, each of which contains one active element. In contrast, ICs typically contain hundreds, thousands, or millions of active elements in a single die.

- **Optoelectronics**—A device that is responsive to or that emits or modifies light waves; for example, LEDs, optical couplers, laser diodes, and photo detectors.

- **Sensors**—A component that provides an electrical signal in response to a specific physical or chemical stimulus, such as heat, pressure, magnetic field, or a particular chemical vapor.

- **Analog**—Integrated circuit realizing analog functions; in analog systems, output signal follows continuously input signal.

- **Micro**—Integrated circuits that are microcomputer related. This category contains three subcategories, that is, microprocessor (MPU), microcontroller (MCU), and digital signal processor (DSP).

USING INDUSTRY ANALYSIS FOR STRATEGIC INTELLIGENCE

- ○ **Microprocessor**—(1) A central processing unit (CPU) fabricated on one or more chips, containing the basic arithmetic, logic, and control elements of a computer that are required for processing data; or (2) an IC that accepts coded instruction, executes the instructions received, and delivers signals that describe its internal status. The instructions may be entered or stored internally.

- ○ **Microcontroller**—A single-chip microcomputer with onboard program ROM and I/O that can be programmed for various control functions.

- ○ **Digital Signal Processor**—Digital circuits used to enhance, analyze, filter, modulate, or otherwise manipulate standard real-world (i.e., analog) functions, such as images, sounds, radar pulses, and other such signals in real-time.

- **Logic**—Integrated circuit performing switching functions; implements logic functions, such as AND, OR, and NOT. Also includes Application Specific Integrated Circuits and Field Programmable Gate Arrays.

- **Memory**—Integrated circuit consisting of memory cells and usually including associated circuits such as those for address selection and amplification. A class of integrated circuits that store digital information, for example, ROM, EPROM, EEPROM, Flash memory, DRAM, and SRAM.

The industry trade press is also a good source of market information. For example, in Figure B.9, *EE Times India* reports the change in semiconductor revenue by end-use from 1995 to 2009. As the figure's title indicates, the only major change in the total available market (TAM) is the incorporation of handheld wireless. The market sectors and percentages have remained relatively steady, which reflects a mature industry. Remember, during this step of building understanding, we are not trying to analyze the semiconductor market and what the above market allocations portend for the industry. It is enough that we understand what major product areas are the buyers of semiconductors.

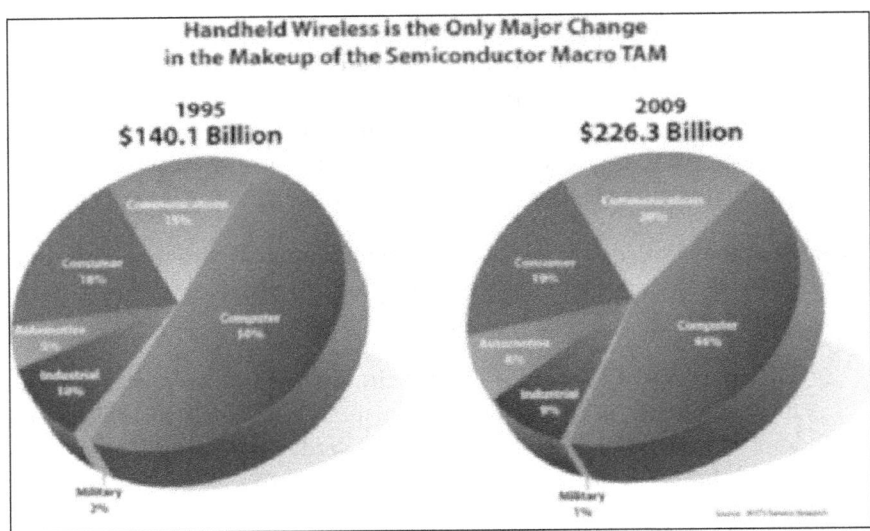

Figure B.9: Semiconductor Total Available Market (TAM) (© Semico Research)[167]

Now that we have looked at the market for semiconductors (power of the buyer), it is also important to understand who are the major producers of semiconductors (intensity of competition). Figure B.10, reported in *EE Times Asia*, shows the top semiconductor vendors ranked by revenue estimates for 2009. These companies will become familiar as information is collected. It is readily apparent that Intel is by far the leading semiconductor producer, with Samsung a distant second, and the remaining companies trailing behind it.

		Top 10 Semiconductor Vendors by Revenue Estimates, 2009 (Millions of U.S. Dollars)				
2009 Rank	2008 Rank	Vendor	2008 Revenue	2009 Revenue	2008–2009 Growth (%)	2009 Market Share (%)
1	1	Intel	34,814	33,253	-4.5	14.6
2	2	Samsung Electronics	17,391	17,686	1.7	7.7
3	3	Toshiba	10,601	9,604	-9.4	4.2
4	4	Texas Instruments	10,593	9,142	-13.7	4.0
5	5	STMicroelectronics	10,270	8,510	-17.1	3.7

USING INDUSTRY ANALYSIS FOR STRATEGIC INTELLIGENCE

Top 10 Semiconductor Vendors by Revenue Estimates, 2009 (Millions of U.S. Dollars) continued							
2009 Rank	2008 Rank	Vendor	2008 Revenue	2009 Revenue	2008–2009 Growth (%)	2009 Market Share (%)
6	8	Qualcomm	6,477	6,409	-1.0	2.8
7	9	Hynix Semiconductor	6,010	6,035	0.4	2.6
8	7	Renesas Technology	7,081	5,670	-19.9	2.5
9	11	Advanced Micro Devices	5,298	5,157	-2.7	2.3
10	6	Infineon Technologies (incl. Qimonda)	8,224	4,682	-43.1	2.1
		Others	138,375	122,223	-11.7	53.5
		Total Market	255,134	228,371	-10.5	100.0

Source: Gartner (March 2010)

Figure B.10: Top 10 Semiconductor Vendors, 2009 (© Gartner, Inc.)[168]

Figure B.11 shows the top ten semiconductor companies projected by 2010 capital investment; the inclusion of the major product line for each company is also useful. For example, Intel is listed as having the largest revenue of semiconductor companies in 2009, and its major product area is listed as MPU, or microprocessor unit. The microprocessor is the main component in the computers that now come in so many forms and sizes. The large revenue numbers reported by Intel are also consistent with the computer sector of the semiconductor market being the largest of the various sectors. Samsung reported the second-largest revenues, and its major product area is memory. While memory is important to the computer sector, memory applications are also present in the consumer, communications, and automotive sectors. There is also a major product category, foundry, which appears on the list. Referring to the value-chain examples in Chapter 2, a foundry is a firm that does not design and produce its own line of semiconductors. The foundry receives the design information and masks from a customer and fabricates the individual die. In some cases, they do not even separate the die from the wafer, and the customer will either complete the packaging of the die or outsource the task to another vendor. The value chain helps to visualize what activities are being discussed in the trade press.

2010 Rank	Company	2007 ($M)	07/06 % Change	2008 ($M)	08/07 % Change	2009 ($M)	09/08 % Change	2010F ($M)	10/09 % Change	Major Product
1	Samsung	7,964	16%	6,750	-15%	3,518	-48%	5,000	42%	Memory
2	Intel	5,000	-13%	5,197	4%	4,515	-13%	4,900	9%	MPU
3	TSMC	2,557	6%	1,877	-27%	2,687	43%	4,800	79%	Foundry
4	Toshiba	3,595	18%	2,210	-39%	950	-57%	1,950	105%	Memory
5	AMD/GlobalFoundries**	1,683	-9%	621	-63%	466	-25%	1,900	308%	MPU/Foundry
6	Hynix	5,145	8%	2,900	-44%	855	-71%	1,840	115%	Memory
7	Micron	3,700	23%	2,300	-38%	800	-65%	1,715	114%	Memory
8	Nanya	2,098	131%	695	-67%	640	-8%	1,415	121%	Memory
9	UMC	850	-15%	349	-59%	551	58%	1,350	145%	Foundry
10	Elpida	2,111	59%	890	-58%	535	-40%	1,000	87%	Memory
	Total	34,703	12%	23,789	-31%	15,517	-35%	25,870	67%	

*Includes company's share of joint-venture spending **Includes Chartered in 2010
Source: IC Insights, Company Reports

Figure B.11: Top 10 Semiconductor Industry Capital Spenders (© IC Insights, Company Reports)[169]

Understanding the size and scope of the market makes it apparent that the semiconductor industry, although mature, is still experiencing growth. It may seem counterintuitive that a mature industry continues to spend large amounts on research and development, but that is because, while the semiconductor process steps are easy to understand, the actual achievement of producing the design is intellectually and capitally intensive. To bring it up to a strategic level, it is also important to note where the leading companies are headquartered and where they are producing their product. This will become apparent as collection begins and will be important in our analysis task. For now, having a list of the key competitors will be useful in the collection and analysis of industry information.

This appendix provides a basic background in the industry we want to analyze. At this point, we have a general overview of semiconductors and the processing of semiconductors into integrated circuits, and insight into the size and composition of the semiconductor market. A test of our understanding is to construct a value chain for the industry. If you have already found one for the industry, use it as a contextual template for the collection and analysis of industry information.

Appendix C

Data Sources Specific to Semiconductor Industry

Books

Since getting the latest data is a primary consideration, it is important to search for recent books on the industry. For example, at the start of research for this study, a 2009 book by Claire Brown and Greg Linden, *Chips and Change*, turned out to be an excellent data source for understanding the origin, development, and future of the semiconductor industry.[170] The book even provides a value chain for the semiconductor industry. A 2008 book on China's high-technology industry, *China's Science and Technology Sector and the Forces of Globalization*, provides an interesting perspective on the prospects and problems for development of China's semiconductor industry.[171]

Reports

The National Academy of Sciences, a nonprofit institution, has a searchable website of its publications, and many are free to download.[172] While the publication dates of National Academy reports are unpredictable, you can request e-mail notifications when topics of interest are available. The federal government, particularly within the Department of Commerce, provides a regular stream of trade and industry statistics, but occasionally they will also produce reports on global trade topics that are of interest. For example, the Bureau of Industry and Security provides current news reports regarding trade issues, and its Defense Industrial Base Programs link provides a list of Defense Industrial Capability and Technology Assessments regarding foreign industrial development that may be of interest.[173]

Trade Associations

The major semiconductor trade association websites provide news and documents, although the frequency of their updates and data available are irregular. The major semiconductor industry trade associations are

- Semiconductor Industry Association (SIA): *www.sia-online.org*.

    They provide an updated factsheet with basic statistics on the worldwide semiconductor market and also provide issue papers regarding global competition.

- Taiwan Semiconductor Industry Association (TSIA): *www.tsia.org.tw/Eng*.
- Japan Electronics and Information Technology Industries Association (JEITA): *www.jeita.or.jp/english*.
- Korea Semiconductor Industry Association (KSIA): *www.ksia.or.kr/eng/main*.
- China Semiconductor Industry Association (CSIA): *www.csia.net.cn*. (Note: website's language is not translated into English.)
- Singapore Semiconductor Industry Association (SSIA): *http://www.ssia.org.sg*.
- Electronic Design Automation Consortium (EDAC): *www.edac.org*.
- Semiconductor Equipment and Materials International (SEMI): *www.semi.org*. SEMI is an international trade association that represents the suppliers to the semiconductor industry. It also includes suppliers to the display and photovoltaic (solar-cell) industries. The SEMI trade shows are held around the world, with each providing insight into the host country's semiconductor industry. The SEMI international standards forum invites members to collaborate on developing standards. The SEMI industry statistics group presents industry forecasts and invites other organizations to also share their forecasts at SEMI events.

Trade Journals

The most useful sources of current information on the semiconductor industry are the industry trade journals. Trade journals are much better sources than government policy announcements and the occasional analytical articles in metropolitan newspapers and business magazines, because many of those stories are not much more than news releases from the subject company. The industry trade journals, on the other hand, are reflective of the global evolution of this industry, and not only carry articles of interest to the technical community, they also provide analysis and forecasts on industry-wide

USING INDUSTRY ANALYSIS FOR STRATEGIC INTELLIGENCE

issues. The semiconductor trade press is not immune to industry competition, though. For example, during this book's preparation, the parent company for the trade journal *Semiconductor International* ceased operations and removed its content from the Internet. The reality of publishing these days makes it important to capture hardcopies of source articles in order to document the sources of analysis. In the semiconductor industry, most of the trade journals are available as Web subscriptions, some without charge, while others charge a small fee for subscribing or downloading full text articles:

- *EE Times Asia*: *www.eetasia.com*.

- *EE Times India*: *www.eetindia.co.in*.

- *Electronic Design News*: *www.edn.com*.

    ○ *Electronic Business*—separate subscription available from EDN.

    ○ *ElectronicNewsToday*—separate subscription available from EDN.

- ElectroIQ—portal for electronics manufacturing: *http://www10.giscafe.com/nbc/articles/1/737191/%3Cem%3Ewww.ElectroIQ.com%3C/em%3E*.

    ○ *Solid State Technology*—digital edition available from ElectroIQ.

- SEMI Newsletters: *www.semi.org*.

    ○ *SEMI Global Update*

    ○ *Semiconductor Manufacturing Newsletter* (simplified Chinese)

- *DigiTimes, www.digitimes.com*—provides news summaries free of charge, but to access full articles requires a subscription.

Other Internet Sources

This category concerns the Internet and its ever-evolving platforms and content. The website YouTube (*www.youtube.com*), although pedestrian to aficionados of social media, still provides good sources of information. Using search terms gained from your study of the industry can yield video clips from news organizations, trade associations, and even companies within the industry.[174]

Blogs and Twitter

The blogs by industry analysts, enthusiasts, or employees are embedded or linked into many of the industry trade journals, and can be a good source of information. The EDA Consortium website has a publications page (*www.edac.org/news_publications.jsp*) that provides a list of links to trade journals, but also provides links to news and blog sites, such as EDACafé (*http://www.edacafe.com*), or individual bloggers, such as EDA Confidential (*www.aycinena.com*).

The use of Twitter by the trade journal *Semiconductor International* is noteworthy, but it only Tweeted links to its journal content. This trial experiment went offline with the demise of that trade journal.

Webcasts and Virtual Conferences

The increasing use of webcasts and virtual conferences provide good real-time sources. Subscriptions to the industry trade journals will lead to announcements of these events. These events offer another avenue for the industry to share information and develop market opportunities. The presenter slides are usually available for download prior to the presentation, or the site allows archival access. Figure C.1 shows a recent *EE Times* virtual conference portal that provides all the trappings of a conference with spaces for the auditorium, exhibition, and business meetings.[175]

Figure C.1: Virtual Conference Portal (© UBM Electronics)

Referencing Figure C.1, in a six-hour conference, the listeners can choose the sessions they want and even interact with the presenter via the portal interface. A visit to the exhibit hall provides a view of kiosks for each company exhibiting. Entering the kiosks, the visitor sees a list of company content, such as product presentations and white papers. The virtual conference remains as an archive on the *EE Times* website, but, as with other Internet sources, it is advisable to download the information before it disappears.

Trade Shows

Trade shows are the best alternative to actually visiting semiconductor companies in other countries. Tradeshows will offer sessions in a variety of areas, and it pays to read the program beforehand to ensure it is not devoted to a sub-industry topic or technical interchange. Also, unless you are multilingual, make sure the session is in English or that simultaneous translation is available. Be sure also to take the time to walk through the exhibit halls and gather literature of interest. One caution is that most corporate booths will require a business card or the signing of a register before they will give out literature. The purpose of the exhibit hall is to generate business leads for the companies, so bring appropriate identification if you want to collect information. As a final note, in the absence of attending the trade show, the trade press usually reports from the show and provides their perspective via the Internet. By way of an example of what is available, the SEMI tradeshows are scheduled a year in advance and occur in a different country each quarter. The SEMI tradeshows provide market forecast presentations, and also offer a copy of the proceedings. The shows provide an outsider's perspective of semiconductor companies (SEMI represents the suppliers to the industry), as well as insight into the future outlook for the industry.

Bibliography

Applied Materials. "What Is Solar Electric Power?" Applied Materials video, 6:33. *http://www.appliedmaterials.com/media-resources/wisep.*

Armour, Norm. "The Innovation Imperative: Toward a New Model for Semiconductor Manufacturing." Presentation at SEMI ISS, Half Moon Bay, CA, January 2010.

ASE Group. "Semi Business Evolution." Presentation by Tien Wu, SEMICON Korea 2010, Seoul, Korea, February 2010.

Aycinena, Peggy. *TSMC: The New Pax Romana.* May 26, 2010. *http://www.aycinena.com/index2/index3/tsmc%20pax%20romana%202010.html.*

Baumol, William J., and Alan S. Blinder. *Economics Principles and Policy.* 7th Edition. Orlando, FL: Dryden Press, 1998.

Berger, Suzanne. *How We Compete: What Companies around the World Are Doing to Make It in Today's Global Economy.* New York: Doubleday, 2006.

Birnbaum, Mark D. *Essential Electronic Design Automation (EDA).* Upper Saddle River, NJ: Prentice Hall, 2004.

Bitran, Gabriel R., Suri Gurumurthi, and Shiou Lin Sam. "The Need for Third-Party Coordination in Supply Chain Governance." *MIT Sloan Management Review* 48, no. 3 (Spring 2007): 30–37.

Bogdanski, Jack. "Obsolescence Management: Another Perspective." *Military Embedded Systems* (January/February 2009). *http://www.mil-embedded.com/articles/id/?3747.*

Boundless. "Overview of Types of Plans and Tools for Planning." May 20, 2014. *https://www.boundless.com/management/strategic-management/the-planning-process/overview-of-types-of-plans-and-tools-for-planning/.*

Bradsher, Keith. "China Drawing High-Tech Research from U.S." *New York Times.* March 17, 2010. *http://www.nytimes.com/2010/03/18/ business/global/18research.html?sq=Applied%20Materials%20 &st=nyt&adxnnl=1&scp=2&adxnnlx=1309464261-clRhmw1kjIyy EagvJFAo7A.*

Bremmer, Ian. *The End of the Free Market.* New York: Portfolio, 2010.

Britton, Phil. *"Integrating Web 2.0 Tools in Your Intelligence Process."* Washington: Strategic and Competitive Intelligence Professionals Professionals Conference, 2010. Comment during lecture.

Brown, Clair, and Greg Linden. *Chips and Change: How Crisis Reshapes the Semiconductor Industry.* Cambridge, MA: MIT Press, 2009.

Bruck, Bob. "Economics and Collaboration Panel." Presentation at SEMI ISS, Half Moon Bay, CA, January 2010.

Business Dictionary. "Industry Analysis." *http://www.businessdictionary.com/ definition/industry-analysis.html.*

Caves, Richard E. *American Industry. Structure, Conduct, Performance.* 7th Edition. Edited by Otto Eckstein. Vol. Foundation of Modern Economics Series. Englewood Cliffs, NJ: Prentice Hall, 1992.

Center for History and New Media, George Mason University. Zotero. *http://www.zotero.org/.*

Chang, Pao-Lang, and Chien-Tzu Tsai. "Finding the niche position-competition strategy of Taiwan's IC design industry." *Technovation* 22, no. 2 (February 2002): 101–11.

Chul-ho, Lee. "[Viewpoint] In China, a Giant Stirs." Korea JoongAng Daily. February 1, 2010. *http://joongangdaily.joins.com/article/view. asp?aid=2916001.*

Clarke, Peter. "TSMC breaks ground on LED lighting wafer fab." *EE Times.* March 25, 2010. *http://www.eetimes.com/electronics-news/4088182/ TSMC-breaks-ground-on-LED-lighting-wafer-fab.*

———. "Winners, losers in 2009 chip vendor ranking." *EE Times Asia.* March 31, 2010. *http://www.eetasia.com/ART_8800602399_480200_NT_72aebd89.HTM.*

Conner, Margery. "Protecting your hardware IP in China: Practical experience." EDN. February 4, 2010. *http://www.edn.com/blog/1470000147/post/650052465.html?nid=2431&rid=16641388.*

Council On Competitiveness. *http://www.compete.org.*

Danne, John. "Semiconductor State of the Industry." Semiconductor Industry Association, March 17, 2010. *http://www.choosetocompete.org/downloads/2010_SOI.pdf.*

Dennis Kunkel Microscopy, Inc. In Northwestern University. "How Small Is Small?" DiscoverNano. *http://www.discovernano.northwestern.edu/whatis/index_html/howsmall_html.*

Dertouzos, Michael L., Richard K. Lester, and Robert M. Solow. *Made in America.* New York: HarperPerennial, 1989.

Economic Development Board. "Facts and Figures." *EDB Singapore.* June 28, 2010. *http://www.edb.gov.sg/edb/sg/en_uk/index/industry_sectors/electronics/facts_and_figures.html.*

Economist. "Economics A–Z." March 25, 2010. *http://www.economist.com/research/economics/alphabetic.cfm?term=economics#economics.*

Economy Watch. *http://www.economywatch.com/world-industries/global-industry.html.*

EDA Consortium. *Where Electronics Begin^{TM}*. *http://www.edac.org/Video/ElectronicsBegins/electronics_begins.jsp.*

EE Times. "Medical System Design Conference." May 20, 2010. *http://vshow.on24.com/vshow/medical?l=en#home.*

EE Times Asia. "Flextronics to build design center in Wuzhong." October 20, 2009. *http://www.eetasia.com/ART_8800587191_480100_NT_ d705de31.HTM?8800033984&8800587191&click_ from=8800033984,9949885433,2009-10-20,EEOL,ARTICLE_ ALERT.*

EE Times China. "Portable medical electronics see big market in China." January 18, 2010. *http://www.eetasia.com/RT_8800595589_499495_ NT_d3e66dac.HTM.*

EE Times India. "Barriers restrict China PV market growth." March 10, 2010. *http://www.eetindia.co.in/ART_8800600232_1800008_NT_ 5347451b.HTM.*

EE Times Korea. "South Korea bets on renewable energy." January 19, 2010. *http://www.eetasia.com/ART_8800595704_765245_NT_32db61a9. HTMclick_from=8800040880,9949885433,2010-01-19,EEOL, ARTICLE_ALERT.*

Fleisher, Craig E., and Babette E. Bensoussan. *Business and Competitive Analysis.* Upper Saddle River, NJ: FT Press, 2007.

———. *Strategic and Competitive Analysis.* Upper Saddle River, NJ: Prentice Hall, 2003.

Friedman, Thomas L. *The World Is Flat.* New York: Farrar, Straus and Giroux, 2005.

———. "A Word from the Wise." *New York Times.* March 2, 2010. *http://www. nytimes.com/2010/03/03/opinion/03friedman.html?ref=intelcorporation.*

Gartner, Inc. "Top 10 Semiconductor Vendors by Revenue Estimates, 2009." In Peter Clarke. "Winners, Losers in 2009 Chip Vendor Ranking." *EE Times Asia.* March 31, 2010. *http://www.eetasia.com/ ART_8800602399_480200_NT_72aebd89.HTM.*

George, Roger Z., and James B. Bruce. *Analyzing Intelligence: Origins, Obstacles, and Innovations.* Washington, DC: Georgetown University Press, 2008.

Gereffi, Gary, John Humphrey, and Timothy Sturgeon. "The Governance of Global Value Chains." *Review of International Political Economy* 12, no. 1 (February 2005): 78–104. *http://www.global-production.com/ scoreboard/resources/sturgeon_2005_governance-of-value-chains.pdf.*

Grant, Robert M. *Contemporary Strategy Analysis.* 5th Edition. Malden, MA: Blackwell Publishing Ltd., 2005.

Haines, Gerald K., and Robert E. Leggett. *Watching the Bear: Essays on CIA's Analysis of the Soviet Union.* Pittsburgh: Government Printing Office, 2003.

Heuer, Richard J. Jr. *Psychology of Intelligence Analysis.* Washington, DC: Center for the Study of Intelligence, 1999.

Hoskisson, Robert E., Michael A. Hitt, and R. Duane Ireland. *Competing for Advantage.* Mason, OH: Thomson South-Western, 2004.

Howe, Charles L. "Semiconductor Value Chain." Industrial College of the Armed Forces. Washington DC, January 2006.

Hwang, Adam. "Taiwan exports hit record in May." *DigiTimes*, June 8, 2010. *http://www.digitimes.com/NewsShow/MailHome.asp?datePublish=2010/ 6/8&pages=VL&seq=200.*

IC Insights. *Glossary of Terms.* 2002–2008. *http://www.icinsights.com/search/? q=Glossary+of+Terms+2002-2008.*

Integrated Circuit Engineering Corporation. "Cost Effective IC Manufacturing 1998–1999." *Smithsonian the Chip Collection.* 1997. *http:// smithsonianchips.si.edu/ice/cd/CEICM/TITLE.pdf.*

Intel. *From Sand to Circuits: How Intel makes integrated circuit chips.* May 21, 2010. *http://www.intel.com/Assets/PDF/General/308301003.pdf.*

———. *Moore's Law: Raising the Bar.* 2005. *http://download.intel.com/museum/ Moores_Law/Printed_Materials/Moores_Law_Backgrounder.pdf.*

International Business Strategies, Inc. "Cost of Participation in Semiconductor Industry Increasing: Impact after 32/28nm." Presentation at SEMI ISS, Half Moon Bay, CA, January 2010.

International Technology Roadmap for Semiconductors. "ITRS 2009 Edition." May 19, 2010. *http://www.itrs.net/Links/2009ITRS/Home2009.htm.*

International Trade Administration. *http://www.trade.gov.*

INVESTOPEDIA. *Economics Basics.* A Forbes Digital Company. March 25, 2010. *http://www.investopedia.com/university/economics/default.asp.*

iSuppli. "New phase of electronics market in 2010s." Presentation by Akira Minamika at SEMICON Japan 2009, SEMI Market Seminar, Chiba, Japan, December 2009.

Johnson, Bob. "The Changing Economics of Moore's Law." Presentation at SEMI ISS, Half Moon Bay, CA, January 2010.

Kogut, Bruce. "Designing Global Strategies: Comparative and Competitive Value-Added Chains." *Sloan Management Review* 26, no. 4 (Summer 1985): 15–28.

Kyodo News International. "Toshiba to set up joint venture in China for chip assembly." November 20, 2009. *http://www.healthtechzone.com/news/2009/11/20/4493943.htm.*

LaPedus, Mark. "Analysis: Change is in the wind at SMIC." *EE Times Asia.* November 12, 2009. *http://www.eetasia.com/ART_8800589303_480100_NT_5bba5b55.HTMclick_from=8800035720,9949885433,2009-11-12,EEOL,ARTICLE_ALERT.*

———. "Analysis: Is IBM turning over key IC tech to China?" *EE Times Asia.* October 21, 2009. *http://www.eetasia.com/ART_8800587281_480200_NT_55620e65.HTM.*

———. "Analysis: UMC needs new strategy." *EE Times Asia.* May 26, 2010. *http://www.eetasia.com/ARTP_8800607794_480200.HTM.*

———. "Freescale expands Chengdu design center." *EE Times Asia*. June 7, 2010. http://www.eetimes.com/electronics-news/4199969/Freescale-expands-Chengdu-design-center.

———. "Korea lags in analog, experts warn." *EE Times*. October 16, 2009. http://www.eetimes.com/news/latest/showArticle.jhtml;jsessionid=NKWPPGLPF1RW1QE1GHOSKHWATMY32JVN?articleID=220601073.

———. "Korea's IC industry seen on shaky ground." *EE Times Asia*. October 20, 2009. http://www.eetimes.com/news/latest/showArticle.jhtml;jsessionid=HCFRU2WD32O4BQE1GHRSKH4ATMY32JVN?articleID=220700489.

———. "Six reasons why Samsung will succeed in foundry biz." *EE Times Asia*. March 3, 2010. http://www.eetasia.com/ART_8800599719_480200_NT_9f869000.HTMclick_from=8800044080,9949885433,2010-03-05,EEOL,ARTICLE_ALERT.

Lee, Ingrid, and Jessie Shen. "Chipbond to raise stake in China affiliate." *DigiTimes*. June 7, 2010. http://www.digitimes.com/NewsShow/MailHome.asp?datePublish=2010/6/7&pages=PD&seq=219.

Liang, Quincy. "Taiwan Courts Chinese Automakers—Possibilities of cross-strait synergy in the automobile industry." CENS.com—Taiwan Economic News. April 6, 2010. http://www.cens.com/cens/html/en/news/news_inner_31883.html.

Lowenthal, Mark M. *Intelligence: From Secrets to Policy*, 4th Edition. Washington, DC: CQ Press, 2009.

Maxfield, Clive "Max," and Kuhoo Goyal Edson. *EDA: Where electronics begins*. Cupertino, CA: KuhooZ, Inc., 2001.

Maxfield, Clive. *Bebop to the Boolean Boogie*. 2nd Edition. Boston, MA: Newnes, 2003.

McGahan, Anita M. *How Industries Evolve*. Boston, MA: Harvard Business School Press, 2004.

McGrath, Dylan. "Canon litho dreams hinge on nanoimprint." *EE Times Asia.* March 16, 2010. *http://www.eetasia.com/ART_8800600815_480200_ NT_982140e7.HTMclick_from=8800044799,9949885433,2010-03- 16,EEOL,ARTICLE_ALERT.*

Mentor Graphics. "Reduced Memory Cost Drives New Architecture and Applications." In Rhines, Walden. "Is consolidation the new game for the IC industry?" *EE Times India.* April 7, 2010. *http://www.eetindia. co.in/ART_8800603040_1800007_NT_b69fec09.HTM.*

Microwave Encyclopedia. Growing Semiconductor Boules. July 3, 2005. *http://www.microwaves101.com/encyclopedia/boules.cfm.*

Minamika, Akira. "New phase of electronics market in 2010s." Presentation at SEMICON Japan 2009, SEMI Market Seminar. Chiba, Japan. December 2009.

Mutschler, Ann Steffora. "IC Insights ups ww IC market forecast to 27%." *EDN.* March 9, 2010. *http://www.edn.com/article/457768-IC_Insights_ ups_ww_IC_market_forecast_to_27_.php.*

National Intelligence Council. "Global Trends 2025: The National Intelligence Council's 2025 Project." Vers. NIC 2008-003. November 2008. *http://www.dni.gov/nic/NIC_2025_project.html.*

Navigant Consulting. "Solar in the New Decade: How Far Can We Go?" Presentation by Paula Mints at SEMI ISS, Half Moon Bay, CA, January 2010.

Nevison, Gary. "China REACH to take effect in October." *EDN.* February 26, 2010. *http://www.edn.com/blog/570000257/post/1300052930. html?nid=3351&rid=16641388.*

Northwestern University, Nanoscale Science and Engineering Center. "How Small Is Small?" Discover Nano. 2005. *http://www.discovernano. northwestern.edu/whatis/index_html/howsmall_html.*

NOVA Electronic Materials. Common Wafer Terminology. May 20, 2010. *http://www.novawafers.com/resources-wafer-terminology.html.*

Office of the Director of National Intelligence. "National Intelligence Strategy of the United States of America." August 2009. *http://www.dni.gov/reports/2009_NIS.pdf.*

Oster, Sharon M. *Modern Competitive Analysis.* New York: Oxford University Press, 1999.

Peng, April. "SMIC Beijing 300mm Fab Reported to Be Planning for Expansion." SEMI. June 1, 2010. *http://www.semi.org/en/MarketInfo/CTR_037308?id=sguna0610.*

PingQing, Liu, Gao Yonghui, and Gu Qiang. "Study on the Upgrading of China Integrated Circuit (IC) Industry Up to the Global Value Chain: A Case Study." *Management Science and Engineering* 1, no. 2 (December 2007): 14–21.

Porter, Michael E. *Competitive Advantage.* New York: Free Press, 1985.

———. *The Competitive Advantage of Nations.* New York: Free Press, 1990.

———. *Competitive Strategy.* New York: Free Press, 1980.

———. "The Five Competitive Forces That Shape Strategy." *Harvard Business Review* (January 2008). *http://hbr.org/2008/01/the-five-competitive-forces-that-shape-strategy/ar/1.*

Rasor, Douglas. "Convergence of Technology and Healthcare." Virtual presentation, *EE Times*, Virtual Conference: Medical System Design, May 20, 2010, *http://www.eetimes.com/medical/.*

Rhines, Walden. "Is consolidation the new game for the IC industry?" *EE Times India*, April 7, 2010. *http://www.eetindia.co.in/ART_8800603040_1800007_NT_b69fec09.HTM.*

Ross, Stephen A., Randolph W. Westerfield, and Jeffrey Jaffe. *Corporate Finance*, 7th Edition. New York: McGraw-Hill, 2005.

Ruzyllo, Jerzy. "Semiconductor Glossary." 2001–2009. *http://www.semi1source.com/glossary/default.asp?whichpage=default.*

SEMATECH. "Acronyms and Abbreviations." 2010. *http://www.sematech.org/publications/acronyms/index.htm.*

SEMI. "Can Government Help High Tech and Spur Economic Growth?" February 2, 2010. *http://www.semi.org/en/MarketInfo/ctr_034251?id=sguna0210.*

———. "Closing the China 'Chip Gap' Creates Long-Term Opportunities for Equipment and Materials Suppliers." June 14, 2010. *http://www.semi.org/en/marketinfo/ctr_033668.*

———. SEMI Industry Research & Statistics. "World Fab Forecast and the Trend of Taiwan Foundry and DRAM Fabs." Presentation by Clark Teng at SEMICON Japan exhibition, Chiba, Japan, December 2009.

Semico Research. "Handheld Wireless Is the Only Major Change in the Makeup of the Semiconductor Macro TAM." In Rhines, Walden. "Is consolidation the New Game for the IC industry?" *EE Times India*. April 7, 2010. *http://www.eetindia.co.in/ART_8800603040_1800007_NT_b69fec09.HTM.*

Semiconductor Industry Association. *The International Technology Roadmap for Semiconductors.* 2009 Edition. Austin, TX: International SEMATECH, 2009. *http://www.itrs.net/Links/2009ITRS/Home2009.htm.*

———. "What is a Semiconductor?" May 20, 2014. *http://semiconductors.org/faq/questions/.*

Siam-Heng, Michael H. "Development of China's Semiconductor Industry: Prospects and Problems." Vol. 13. In Elspeth Thompson and Jon Sigurdson. *China's Science and Technology Sector and the Forces of Globalization,* 219. Singapore: World Scientific Publishing, 2008.

Singh, Dinesh Pratap. "Dinesh Pratap Singh's Visualization for Porter's Value Chain." August 5, 2009. *http://commons.wikimedia.org/wiki/File:Porter_Value_Chain.png.*

Shu-yuan, Lin and Wu, Sofia. "Taiwan Conditionally Broadens High-tech Investment in China." Central News Agency (CNA). February 10, 2010. *http://www.etaiwannews.com/etn/news_content.php?id=1177917&lang=eng_news&cate_img=35.jpg&cate_rss=news_Business*.

Song, Young S., Nghis Nguyen, Kei Wong, Eyad Fanous, Eyad Wong, Hanna Kimj, and Steven Hsu. "Silicon Manufacturing." *EE 4345—Semiconductor Electronics Design Project. 2002. www.uta.edu/roncl4345sp02/lectures/L09a_4345_Sp02.ppt*.

Sperling, Ed. "Why the Chartered Semiconductor Acquisition Matters." System-Level Design. October 16, 2009. *http://chipdesignmag.com/sld/sperling/2009/09/11/why-the-chartered-semiconductor-acquisition-matters/*.

Spiegel, Rob. "Manufacturing trending away from China." *EDN*. October 13, 2009. *http://www.edn.com/article/CA6701633.html*.

Strategic and Competitive Intelligence Professionals. FAQ. *http://www.scip.org/resources/content.cfm?itemnumber=601&navItemNumber=533*.

Sturgeon, Timothy J. "Exploring the Risks of Value Chain Modularity: Electronics Outsourcing during the Industry Cycle of 1992–2002." MIT Industrial Performance Center Working Paper Series. May 2003. *http://web.mit.edu/ipc/publications/pdf/03-002.pdf*.

———. "From Commodity Chains to Value Chains: Interdisciplinary Theory Building in an Age of Globalization." MIT Industrial Performance Center Working Paper Series. January 2008. *http://web.mit.edu/ipc/publications/pdf/08-001.pdf*.

———. "How Do We Define Value Chains and Production Networks?" MIT Industrial Performance Center Working Paper Series. April 2001. *http://www.inti.gob.ar/cadenasdevalor/Sturgeon.pdf*.

———. "How Globalization Drives Institutional Diversity: The Japanese Electronics Industry's Response to Value Chain Modularity." *Journal of East Asian Studies* 7 (2007): 1–34.

Suutari, Raymond. *Understanding Industry Structure.* CMA Management. January 2000. *http://findarticles.com/p/articles/mi_hb6419/is_11_73/ai_n28765036/?tag=content;col1.*

Taiwan Semiconductor Industry Association. "Overview on Taiwan IC Industry—2009 Edition." *http://www.tsia.org.tw/Eng/service/publication_more.asp?zvpWnp.*

T@iwan Today. "Ban List for Mainland-Bound Investment Revised." Taiwan's Government Information Office e-publication. February 10, 2010. *http://www.taiwantoday.tw/ct.asp?xitem=94165&CtNode=415.*

TechTerms.Com. "Integrated Circuit." May 21, 2010. *http://www.techterms.com/definition/integratedcircuit.*

Tokyo Electron. "TEL's Views on Equipment Maker Future Business." Presentation by Ken Sato at SEMI ISS, Half Moon Bay, CA, January 2010.

Top-Alternative-energy-sources.com. "The Czochralski Process." May 20, 2014. *http://www.top-alternative-energy-sources.com/Czochralski-process.html.*

Torrance, Randy. "IC reverse engineering—a design team perspective." *EDN.* March 11, 2010. *http://www.edn.com/design/integrated-circuit-design/4312346/IC-reverse-engineering-a-design-team-perspective.*

Tseng, Clark. "LED Industry Set to Enter Fast Growth Stage in 2010: New Investments, New Market Entrants." SEMI. *http://www.semi.org/en/IndustrySegments/LED/CTR_035763?id=sguna0410.*

UBM Electronics. "Enjoy the Show." Image screenshot. *EE Times* Virtual Conference: Medical System Design. May 20, 2010. *http://www.eetimes.com/medical/.*

Van Opstal, Debra. *The Resilient Economy: Integrating Competitiveness and Security.* Council on Competitiveness. July 2007. *http://www.compete.org/publications/detail/31/the-resilient-economy-integrating-competitiveness-and-security/.*

Vardaman, Jan, and Dan Tracy. "Japanese Companies Continue to Dominate the Packaging Materials Market." SEMI. January 5, 2010. *http://www. semi.org/en/MarketInfo/PackagingMarket/ctr_033627?id=sgurow0110.*

VLSI Research. "Economics and Collaboration Panel Discussion." Panel presentation at SEMI ISS, Half Moon Bay, CA, January 2010.

Waldron, Anna M., and Carl A. Batt. "How Small Am I? The Science of Nanotechnology." *PBS NewsHour Extra.* 2010. *http://www.pbs.org/ newshour/extra/teachers/lessonplans/science/nanotechnology.html.*

Wang, Hsiao-wen. "Why TSMC Showed Mercy." *CommonWealth Magazine.* February 4, 2010. *http://english.cw.com.tw/article.do?action =show &id=11727.*

Wilson, Ron. "Semiconductors, emerging markets, and self-interest of survival." *EDN.* November 20, 2009. *http://www.edn.com/blog/1690000169/ post/1770050777.html?nid=3357&rid=16641388.*

World Semiconductor Trade Statistics. "WSTS Semiconductor Market Forecast Autumn 2009." November 17, 2009. *http://www.wsts.org/ PRESS/PRESS-ARCHIVE/WSTS-Semiconductor-Market-Forecast-Autumn-2009.*

Yoshida, Junko. "New Renesas chief shares renaissance roadmap." *EE Times Asia.* May 24, 2010. http://www.eetasia.com/ARTP_ 8800607528_499495. HTM.

Zakaria, Fareed. *The Post-American World.* New York: W. W. Norton & Company Inc., 2008.

NOTES

1 While the Council on Competitiveness is not the only voice on these issues, it provides an open-source forum on national competitiveness and concomitant issues.

2 Thomas L. Friedman's books, including *The World Is Flat* (New York: Farrar, Straus and Giroux, 2005) and its follow-on editions, provide a good overview of the impact of global Internet connectivity and the diffusion of knowledge it enables.

3 Based on my reading of "The National Intelligence Strategy," Director of National Intelligence (DNI), August 2009.

4 Suzanne Berger, *How We Compete: What Companies around the World Are Doing to Make It in Today's Global Economy* (New York: Doubleday, 2006), 9.

5 Gerald K. Haines and Robert E. Leggett, *Watching the Bear: Essays on CIA's Analysis of the Soviet Union* (Pittsburgh: Government Printing Office, 2003), 17.

6 Ibid., 18.

7 Ibid., 21.

8 Ibid., 17.

9 Dertouzos et al., *Made in America*, 1.

10 Mark M. Lowenthal, *Intelligence: From Secrets to Policy*, 4th Edition (Washington, DC: CQ Press, 2009), 267. (Since this observation was made, the source was released in a 5th edition.) The compelling questions can be synopsized as protecting intelligence sources and methods, determining distribution rules for intelligence gathered, and whether there was an implicit quid pro quo from the government providing intelligence to business.

11 Berger, *How We Compete*, 290–91.

12 Based on my reading of the "National Intelligence Strategy," DNI, August 2009.

13 Fareed Zakaria, *The Post-American World* (New York: W. W. Norton & Company, 2008), 4.

14 DNI, "National Intelligence Strategy," 5.

15 Ibid.

16 DNI, "National Intelligence Strategy," 3–4.

17 National Intelligence Council. *Global Trends 2025: A Transformed World*, November 2008, iv. This observation was listed under the heading "Relative Certainty."

18 Timothy J. Sturgeon, "How Do We Define Value Chains and Production Networks?" MIT Industrial Performance Center Working Paper Series, April 2001, *http://www.inti.gob.ar/cadenasdevalor/Sturgeon.pdf.*

19 Industry analysis definition adapted from *Business Dictionary, http://www.businessdictionary.com/definition/industry-analysis.html.*

20 Anita M. McGahan, *How Industries Evolve* (Boston, MA: Harvard Business School Press, 2004), 7.

21 Adapted (with permission) from Stephen A. Ross, Ronald W. Westerfield, and Jeffrey Jaffe, *Corporate Finance*, 7th ed. (New York: McGraw-Hill, 2005), Figure 1.4.

22 Strategic and Competitive Intelligence Professionals, a leading industry nonprofit organization, defines competitive intelligence "as a necessary, ethical business discipline for decision making based on understanding the competitive environment." Strategic and Competitive Intelligence Professionals FAQ, *http://www.scip.org/re_pdfs/1395928684_pdf_FrequentlyAskedQuestions.pdf.*

23 Robert M. Grant, *Contemporary Strategy Analysis*, 5th ed. (Malden, MA: Blackwell Publishing Ltd., 2005), 113.

24 Michael E. Porter, *Competitive Strategy* (New York: Free Press, 1980).

25 Robert E. Hoskisson, Michael A. Hitt, and R. Duane Ireland, *Competing for Advantage* (Mason, OH: Thomson South-Western, 2004), 82.

26 Adapted (with permission) from Michael E. Porter, "The Five Competitive Forces That Shape Strategy," *Harvard Business Review* (January 2008), *http://hbr.org/2008/01/the-five-competitive-forces-that-shape-strategy/ar/1.*

27 The word *environment* is not meant to connote a focus on the impact of "green" or "eco-friendly" factors on an industry.

28 Craig S. Fleisher and Babette E. Bensoussan, *Business and Competitive Analysis* (Upper Saddle River, NJ: FT Press, 2007), 88.

29 Boundless, "Overview of Types of Plans and Tools for Planning," May 20, 2014, *https://www.boundless.com/management/strategic-management/the-planning-process/overview-of-types-of-plans-and-tools-for-planning/.*

30 Fleisher and Bensoussan, *Business and Competitive Analysis*, 88.

31 Adapted (with permission) from Robert E. Hoskisson, Michael A. Hitt, and R. Duane Ireland, *Competing for Advantage* (Mason, OH: Thomson South-Western, 2004), Figure 3.1.

32 Michael E. Porter, *Competitive Advantage* (New York: Free Press, 1985).

33 Dinesh Pratap Singh, "Dinesh Pratap Singh's Visualization for Porter's Value Chain," August 5, 2009, *http://commons.wikimedia.org/wiki/File:Porter_Value_Chain.png*.

34 Timothy Sturgeon, "How Do We Define Value Chains and Production Networks?," MIT Industrial Performance Center Working Paper Series, April 2001, *http://www.inti.gob.ar/cadenasdevalor/Sturgeon.pdf*.

35 Gary Gereffi, John Humphrey, and Timothy Sturgeon, "The Governance of Global Value Chains," *Review of International Political Economy* 12, no. 1 (February 2005): Figure 1. Reprinted with permission of the authors and Taylor & Francis Group, *http://www.global-production.com/scoreboard/resources/sturgeon_2005_governance-of-value-chains.pdf*.

36 Michael E. Porter, *Competitive Strategy* (New York: Free Press, 1980), 158.

37 Anita M. McGahan, *How Industries Evolve* (Boston, MA: Harvard Business School Press, 2004), 67.

38 "Global Industry," *Economy Watch*, *http://www.economywatch.com/world-industries/global-industry.html*.

39 International Trade Administration, *http://www.trade.gov/*.

40 International Trade Administration, "U.S. Export Fact Sheet," *http://trade.gov/press/press_releases/2009/export-factsheet_031309.pdf*.

41 The NAICS code specifies industries by the type of product or service they produce.

42 Berger, *How We Compete*, 78–79.

43 Adapted (with permission) based on graphic provided by the Taiwan Semiconductor Industry Association. For more information, see "Overview on Taiwan IC Industry—2009 Edition," *http://www.tsia.org.tw/Uploads/Publications/2012%20Overview-Final.pdf*.

44 Adapted (with permission) from Pao-Lang Chang and Chien-Tzu Tsai, "Finding the niche position-competition strategy of Taiwan's IC design industry," Technovation 22, no. 2 (February 2002): Figure 1.

45 Charles L. Howe, "Semiconductor Value Chain," Industrial College of the Armed Forces, Washington, DC, January 2006.

46 Ibid.

47 Timothy Sturgeon, "How Do We Define Value Chains and Production Networks?" MIT Industrial Performance Center Working Paper Series. April 2001, *http://www.inti.gob.ar/cadenasdevalor/Sturgeon.pdf*.

48 The term "daily scrape" comes from an open-source analyst who shared his method for reviewing and saving articles of interest from the daily newspapers from the target country.

49 Zotero was developed by the Center for History and New Media at George Mason University. The program is available for download at: *http://www.zotero.org/*.

50 Zotero supports many citation formats.

51 Richard J. Heuer's book, *Psychology of Intelligence Analysis* (Washington, DC: Center for the Study of Intelligence, 1999), is an excellent source for this topic.

52 Personal notes from "SEMI ISS Blue Chip Panel," SEMI Industry Strategic Symposium, Half Moon Bay, CA, January 2010.

53 Adapted (with permission) from Norm Armour, "The Innovation Imperative: Toward a New Model for Semiconductor Manufacturing," presentation at the SEMI Industry Strategic Symposium, Half Moon Bay, CA, January 2010, slide 20.

54 International Business Strategies, Inc., "Cost of Participation in Semiconductor Industry Increasing: Impact after 32/28nm," presentation at SEMI Industry Strategic Symposium, Half Moon Bay, CA, January 2010, slide 17 (reprinted with permission).

55 Ibid., slide 11.

56 VLSI Research, "Economics and Collaboration Panel Discussion," SEMI Industry Strategic Symposium, Half Moon Bay, CA, January 2010, slide 7 (adapted and reprinted with permission).

57 "Fabless Companies Gain in Top 20 Ranking," Semiconductor International, March 3, 2009 (adapted and reprinted with permission).

58 Dick James, "Apple's A4 iPad chip is Samsung 45-nm," *Semiconductor International*, April 12, 2010.

59 Randy Torrance and Dick James, "IC reverse engineering—a design team perspective," *Electronics Design Network,* March 11, 2010, *http://www.edn.com/design/integrated-circuit-design/4312346/IC-reverse-engineering-a-design-team-perspective.*

60 Walden Rhines, "Is Consolidation the New Game for the IC Industry?" *EE Times India*, April 7, 2010, *http://www.eetindia.co.in/ART_8800603040_1800007_NT_b69fec09.HTM.*

61 Akira Minamika, "New phase of electronics market in 2010s" presentation, market seminar, SEMICON Japan 2009, Tokyo, Japan, December 2009, slide 30.

62 John Daane, "Semiconductor State of the Industry," Semiconductor Industry

Association, March 17, 2010, *http://www.choosetocompete.org/downloads/2010_SOI.pdf*.

63 Ann Steffora Mutschler, "IC Insights ups ww IC market forecast to 27%," *Electronics Design Network*, March 9, 2010, *http://www.edn.com/article/457768-IC_Insights_ups_ww_IC_market_forecast_to_27_.php*.

64 Tokyo Electron, "TEL's Views on Equipment Maker Future Business," presentation by Ken Sato, SEMI Industry Strategic Symposium, Half Moon Bay, CA, January 2010, slide 9.

65 Ron Wilson, "Semiconductors, emerging markets, and self-interest of survival," *Electronics Design Network*, November 20, 2009, *http://www.edn.com/blog/1690000169/post/1770050777.html?nid=3357&rid=16641388*.

66 Tokyo Electron, "TEL's Views on Equipment Maker Future Business."

67 Bob Johnson, "The Changing Economics of Moore's Law," presentation at SEMI Industry Strategic Symposium, Half Moon Bay, CA, January 2010, slide 8.

68 Clair Brown and Greg Linden, *Chips and Change: How Crisis Reshapes the Semiconductor Industry* (Cambridge, MA: MIT Press, 2009), 44.

69 Berger, *How We Compete*, 78–82. Berger provides a good description of modularity in the semiconductor industry.

70 Brown and Linden, *Chips and Change*, 45.

71 SEMI Industry Research & Statistics, "World Fab Forecast and the Trend of Taiwan Foundry and DRAM Fabs," presentation by Clark Teng, SEMICON Japan, Chiba, Japan, December 2009, slide 23 (adapted and reprinted with permission).

72 Adapted (with permission) from Applied Materials, "What Is Solar Electric Power," Applied Materials video, 6:33, *http://www.appliedmaterials.com/media-resources/wisep*.

73 Navigant Consulting, "Solar in the New Decade: How Far Can We Go?" presentation by Paula Mints, SEMI Industry Strategic Symposium, Half Moon Bay, CA, January 2010, slide 15 (adapted and reprinted with permission).

74 David Lammers, "LED Manufacturing Tools Gain Attention," *Semiconductor International*, January 26, 2010.

75 Yole Développement, "HB LED & LED Packaging 2009," October 2009: also, "LED Manufacturing Steps," reprinted in David Lammers, "LED Manufacturing Tools Gain Attention," *Semiconductor International*, January 26, 2010 (reprinted here with permission).

76 iSuppli, "New phase of electronics market in 2010s," presentation by Akira Minamika, SEMICON Japan, SEMI market seminar, Chiba, Japan, December 2009, slide 30 (adapted and reprinted with permission).

77 Clark Tseng, "LED Industry Set to Enter Fast Growth Stage in 2010: New Investments, New Market Entrants," SEMI, April 6, 2010, *http://www.semi.org/en/IndustrySegments/LED/CTR_035763?id=sguna0410* (adapted and reprinted with permission).

78 Douglas Rasor, "Convergence of Technology and Healthcare," virtual presentation, EE Times, Medical System Design Virtual Conference, May 20, 2010, http://www.eetimes.com/medical/, slide 3 (adapted and reprinted with permission).

79 Personal notes from SEMICON Korea, Seoul, Korea, February 4, 2010.

80 ASE Group, "Semi Business Evolution," presentation by Tien Wu, SEMICON Korea 2010, Seoul, Korea, February 2010, slide 20 (reprinted with permission).

81 Douglas Rasor, "Convergence of Technology and Healthcare," virtual presentation, *EE Times*, Medical System Design Virtual Conference, May 20, 2010, *http://www.eetimes.com/medical/*, slide 23 (reprinted with permission).

82 See Berger, *How We Compete*, 78–79; also, Brown and Linden, *Chips and Change*, 197. Mark LaPedus, "Korea's IC industry seen on shaky ground," *EE Times*, October 20, 2009, *http://www.eetimes.com/news/latest/showArticle.jhtml;jsessionid=HCFRU2WD32O4BQE1GHRSKH4ATMY32JVN?articleID=220700489*. Ed Sperling, "Why the Chartered Semiconductor Acquisition Matters," System-Level Design, October 16, 2009, *http://chipdesignmag.com/sld/sperling/2009/09/11/why-the-chartered-semiconductor-acquisition-matters/*; SEMI, "Can Government Help High Tech and Spur Economic Growth?" February 2, 2010, *http://www.semi.org/en/MarketInfo/ctr_034251?id=sguna0210*.

83 Brown and Linden, *Chips and Change*, 37.

84 Brown and Linden, *Chips and Change*, 27; Junko Yoshida, "New Renesas chief shares renaissance roadmap," *EE Times Asia*, May 24, 2010, *http://www.eetasia.com/ARTP_8800607528_499495.HTM*.

85 Kenji Tsuda, "Japan's IC Makers to Consolidate Fabs," *Semiconductor International*, February 2, 2009; "Toshiba to Set Up Joint Venture in China for Chip Assembly," Kyodo News International, Kyodo, November 20, 2009, *http://satellite.tmcnet.com/news/2009/11/20/4493943.htm*.

86 "Pretax Earnings Improve at 7 Japan Chipmaking Gear Makers," *Semiconductor International*, February 15, 2010.

87 Dylan McGrath, "Canon Litho Dreams Hinge on Nanoimprint," *EE Times Asia*, March 16, 2010, *http://www.eetasia.com/ART_8800600815_480200_NT_982140e7. HTMclick_from=8800044799,9949885433,2010-03-16,EEOL,ARTICLE_ALERT.* The world's largest lithography company is AML Holding NV of the Netherlands.

88 Jan Vardaman and Dan Tracy, "Japanese Companies Continue to Dominate the Packaging Materials Market," SEMI, January 5, 2010, *http://www.semi.org/en/ MarketInfo/PackagingMarket/ctr_033627?id=sgurow0110.*

89 Akira Minamika, "New phase of electronics market in 2010s," presentation at SEMICON Japan 2009, SEMI Market Seminar, Chiba, Japan, December 2009, 30.

90 Mark LaPedus, "Korea's IC industry seen on shaky ground," October 20, 2009; Mark LaPedus, "Korea lags in analog, experts warn," *EE Times*, October 16, 2009, *http://www.eetimes.com/news/latest/showArticle.jhtml;jsessionid=NKWPP GLPF1RW1QE1GHOSKHWATMY32JVN?articleID=220601073*; Lee Chul-ho, "[Viewpoint] In China, a Giant Stirs," Korea JoongAng Daily, February 1, 2010, *http://joongangdaily.joins.com/article/view.asp?aid=2916001.*

91 Vardaman and Tracy, "Japanese Companies Continue to Dominate the Packaging Materials Market," SEMI, January 5, 2010.

92 LaPedus, "Korea's IC industry seen on shaky ground," October 20, 2009.

93 LaPedus, "Korea lags in analog, experts warn," October 16, 2009.

94 Dick James, "Apple's A4 iPad chip is Samsung 45-nm," *Semiconductor International*, April 12, 2010; Mark LaPedus, "Six reasons why Samsung will succeed in foundry biz," *EE Times Asia*, March 3, 2010, *http://www.eetasia.com/ART_8800599719_480200_ NT_9f869000.HTMclick_from=8800044080,9949885433,2010-03- 05,EEOL,ARTICLE_ALERT.*

95 "South Korea bets on renewable energy," *EE Times Asia*, January 19, 2010, *http://www.eetasia.com/ART_8800595704_765245_NT_32db61a9.HTMclick_ from=8800040880,9949885433,2010-01-19,EEOL,ARTICLE_ALERT.*

96 Economic Development Board, "EDB Singapore," June 28, 2010, *http://www. edb.gov.sg/edb/sg/en_uk/index/industry_sectors/electronics/facts_and_figures.html.*

97 Business Wire, "Applied Materials Opens Global Hub in Singapore for Manufacturing Semiconductor Equipment," *Semiconductor International*, April 13, 2010.

98 Ed Sperling, "Why the Chartered Semiconductor Acquisition Matters," System-Level Design, October 16, 2009, *http://chipdesignmag.com/sld/sperling/2009/09/11/ why-the-chartered-semiconductor-acquisition-matters/.*

99 IC Insights, "2009 Major IC Foundries," in "TSMC Maintains Top Spot Among Foundries," *Semiconductor International*. January 28, 2010 (adapted and reprinted with permission).

100 Mark LaPedus, "UMC needs new strategy," *EE Times Asia*, May 26, 2010, *http://www.eetasia.com/ARTP_8800607794_480200.HTM*.

101 Peggy Aycinena, "TSMC: The New Pax Romana," EDA Confidential, May 26, 2010, *http://www.aycinena.com/index2/index3/tsmc%20pax%20romana%20 2010.html*.

102 Market News Publishing, "And MAPPER Reached Joint Development Milestone," *Semiconductor International*, February 19, 2010.

103 Peter Clarke, "TSMC breaks ground on LED lighting wafer fab," *EE Times*, March 25, 2010, *http://www.eetimes.com/electronics-news/4088182/TSMC-breaks-ground-on-LED-lighting-wafer-fab*.

104 Akira Minamika, "New phase of electronics market in 2010s," presentation at SEMICON Japan 2009 SEMI, Market Seminar, Chiba, Japan, December 2009, slide 30 (adapted and reprinted with permission).

105 "Taiwan Legislature Rejects DRAM Industry Restructuring Plan," *Semiconductor International*, November 12, 2009.

106 "Taiwan Tax Cut Agreement Expected to Benefit Businesses," Osc Seoul Yonhap in English, January 14, 2010.

107 Lin Shu-yuan and Sofia Wu, "Taiwan Conditionally Broadens High-tech Investment In China," *Central News Agency* (CNA), February 10, 2010, *http://www.etaiwannews.com/etn/news_content.php?id=1177917&lang=eng_news&cate_img=35.jpg&cate_rss=news_Business;* "Ban List for Mainland-Bound Investment Revised," T@iwan Today, February 10, 2010, *http://www.taiwantoday.tw/ct.asp?xitem =94165&CtNode=415*.

108 Ibid.

109 "Flextronics to build design center in Wuzhong," *EE Times Asia*, October 20, 2009, *http://www.eetasia.com/ART_8800587191_480100_NT_d705de31. HTM?8800033984&8800587191&click_from=8800033984,9949885433,2009-10-20,EEOL,ARTICLE_ALERT*.

110 Lin Shu-yuan and Sofia Wu, "Taiwan Conditionally Broadens High-tech Investment In China," *CAN*, October 20, 2009.

111 Asia Pulse, "Taiwanese Chip Foundries Investing in Chinese Firms," *Semiconductor International*, April 5, 2010.

112 David Lammers, "TSMC to Take No Day-to-Day Role in SMIC," *Semiconductor International*, November 11, 2009; China Knowledge Newswire, "TSMC says no plans to move advanced plants to mainland," *Semiconductor International*, April 7, 2010.

113 Ingrid Lee and Jessie Shen, "Chipbond to raise stake in China affiliate," *DigiTimes*, June 7, 2010, *http://www.digitimes.com/NewsShow/MailHome.asp?datePublish =2010/6/7&pages=PD&seq=219*.

114 Quincy Liang, "Taiwan Courts Chinese Automakers—Possibilities of cross-strait synergy in the automobile industry," CENS.com—The Taiwan Economic News, April 6, 2010, *http://www.cens.com/cens/html/en/news/news_inner_31883.html*.

115 Adam Hwang, "Taiwan exports hit record in May," *DigiTimes*, June 8, 2010, *http://www.digitimes.com/NewsShow/MailHome.asp?datePublish=2010/6/8&pages= VL&seq=200*.

116 April Peng, "SMIC Beijing 300mm Fab Reported to Be Planning for Expansion," SEMI, June 1, 2010, available at *http://www.semi.org/en/MarketInfo/ CTR_037308?id=sguna0610* (reprinted with permission from SEMI).

117 "Closing the China 'Chip Gap' Creates Long-Term Opportunities for Equipment and Materials Suppliers," SEMI, June 14, 2010, *http://www.semi.org/ en/marketinfo/ctr_033668*.

118 Hsiao-wen Wang, "Why TSMC Showed Mercy," *CommonWealth Magazine*, February 4, 2010, *http://english.cw.com.tw/article.do?action=show&id=11727*.

119 Mark LaPedus, "Analysis: Change is in the wind at SMIC," *EE Times Asia*, November 12, 2009, *http://www.eetasia.com/ART_8800589303_480100_NT_5bba5b55. HTMclick_from=8800035720,9949885433,2009-11-12,EEOL,ARTICLE_ ALERT*.

120 VLSI Research, "TSMC & SMIC Profitability," in "China Leads World Out of Recession, Through Recovery," *Semiconductor International*, January 14, 2010.

121 LaPedus, "Analysis: Change is in the wind at SMIC," November 12, 2009.

122 "China IC Industry Development Targets Renewed and Repurposed Fabs," Targeted News Service, March 8, 2010.

123 Margery Conner, "Protecting your hardware IP in China: Practical experience," *Electronics Design Network*, February 4, 2010, *http://www.edn.com/blog/1470000147/ post/650052465.html?nid=2431&rid=16641388*.

124 Hsiao-wen Wang, "Why TSMC Showed Mercy," *CommonWealth Magazine*, February 4, 2010.

125 Mark LaPedus, "Analysis: Is IBM turning over key IC tech to China?" *EE Times Asia*, October 21, 2009, http://www.eetasia.com/ART_8800587281_480200_NT_55620e65.HTM.

126 Mark LaPedus, "Freescale expands Chengdu design center," *EE Times Asia*, June 7, 2010, http://www.eetimes.com/electronics-news/4199969/Freescale-expands-Chengdu-design-center.

127 "Intel Capital and China Investment Corporation Announce Collaboration Agreement," *Semiconductor International*, February 12, 2010.

128 Keith Bradsher, "China Drawing High-Tech Research from U.S.," *New York Times*, March 17, 2010, http://www.nytimes.com/2010/03/18/business/global/18research.html?sq=Applied%20Materials%2 &st=nyt&adxnnl=1&scp=2&adxnnlx=1309464261-clRhmw1kjIyyEagvJFAo7A.

129 Ibid.

130 Thomas L. Friedman, "A Word from the Wise," *New York Times*, March 2, 2010, http://www.nytimes.com/2010/03/03/opinion/03friedman.html?ref=intelcorporation.

131 "Elpida Plans China, Taiwan Factories to Meet Demand," *Business Week*, June 7, 2010.

132 Rob Spiegel, "Manufacturing trending away from China," *Electronics Design Network*, October 13, 2009, http://www.edn.com/article/CA6701633.html.

133 Personal notes from SEMI ISS Blue Chip Panel, SEMI Industry Strategic Symposium, Half Moon Bay, CA, January 2010.

134 Gary Nevison, "China REACH to take effect in October," *Electronics Design Network*, February 26, 2010, http://www.edn.com/blog/570000257/post/1300052930.html?nid=3351&rid=16641388.

135 "Barriers restrict China PV market growth," *EE Times India*, March 10, 2010, http://www.eetindia.co.in/ART_8800600232_1800008_NT_5347451b.HTM.

136 Research in China, "China Polysilicon Industry Report, 2009" in "China Looks to Control Polysilicon Oversupply, Quality," PV Society, December 3, 2009 (reprinted with permission).

137 "Portable medical electronics see big market in China," *EE Times Asia*, January 18, 2010, http://www.eetasia.com/ART_8800595589_499495_NT_d3e66dac.HTM.

138 Ian Bremmer, *The End of the Free Market* (New York: Portfolio, 2010), 149.

139 The economics of industry is being highlighted here; based on the 2009 NIS, the intelligence community is adept at analyzing monetary policy, exchange rates, capital flows, and other major macroeconomic trends.

140 Bremmer, *The End of the Free Market*, 23.

141 Sperling, "Why the Chartered Semiconductor Acquisition Matters."

142 Bremmer, *The End of the Free Market*, 5.

143 Ibid., 175.

144 Ibid., 199.

145 Adapted from Robert E. Hoskisson, Michael A. Hitt, and R. Duane Ireland, *Competing for Advantage* (Mason, OH: Thomson South-Western, 2004), Figure 3.1 (adapted with permission).

146 IC Insights, "Glossary of Terms, 2002–2008," *http://www.icinsights.com/search/?q=Glossary+of+Terms+2002-2008*.

147 Semiconductor Industry Association, "What is a Semiconductor?," May 20, 2014, *http://semiconductors.org/faq/questions/*.

148 Jack Bogdanski, "Obsolescence Management: Another Perspective," Military Embedded Systems, January/February 2009, *http://www.mil-embedded.com/articles/id/?3747*.

149 Brown and Linden, *Chips and Change*, 9.

150 Visualizations of this common industry process can be found in Top-Alternative-energy-sources.com, "The Czochralski Process," May 20, 2014, *http://www.top-alternative-energy-sources.com/Czochralski-process.html*; and in corporate websites, for example, SUMCO Corporation, "The Next Generation Wafer," May 17, 2010, *http://www.sumcosi.com/english/products/next_generation/breakthrough.html*.

151 NOVA Electronic Materials, "Common Wafer Terminology," May 20, 2010, *http://www.novawafers.com/resources-wafer-terminology.html*.

152 Microwave Encyclopedia, "Growing Semiconductor Boules," July 3, 2005, *http://www.microwaves101.com/encyclopedia/boules.cfm*.

153 SEMATECH, "Acronyms and Abbreviations," *http://www.sematech.org/publications/acronyms/index.htm*.

154 Definition of integrated circuit is adapted from TechTerms.Com, May 21, 2010, *http://www.techterms.com/definition/integratedcircuit*.

155 Intel, "Moore's Law: Raising the Bar," 2005, *http://www.bandwidthco.com/whitepapers/hardware/cpu/moore/Moores%20Law%20-%20Raising%20the%20Bar.pdf*.

156 Adapted (with permission) from Mentor Graphics, "Reduced Memory Cost Drives New Architecture and Applications," in "Is consolidation the new game

for the IC industry?," *EE Times India*, April 7, 2010, *http://www.eetindia.co.in/ART_8800603040_1800007_NT_b69fec09.HTM*.

157 Semiconductor Industry Association, The International Technology Roadmap for Semiconductors, 2009 Edition. International SEMATECH: Austin, TX (2009). *http://www.itrs.net/Links/2009ITRS/Home2009.htm* (adapted and reprinted with permission).

158 Northwestern University, Nanoscale Science and Engineering Center, "How Small Is Small?," DiscoverNano, 2005, *http://www.discovernano.northwestern.edu/whatis/index_html/howsmall_html* (reprinted with permission from Northwestern University and Dennis Kunkel Microscopy, Inc.); Anna M. Waldron and Carl A. Batt, "How Small Am I? The Science of Nanotechnology," PBS NewsHour Extra, 2010, *http://www.pbs.org/newshour/extra/teachers/lessonplans/science/nanotechnology.html* (reprinted with permission from PBS NewsHour/MacNeil-Lehrer Productions).

159 "Where Electronics Begin," EDA Consortium, *http://www.edac.org/Video/ElectronicsBegins/electronics_begins.jsp*.

160 For a good overview of the process, see "From Sand to Circuits: How Intel makes integrated circuit chips," Intel, May 21, 2010, *http://www.intel.com/Assets/PDF/General/308301003.pdf*.

161 Integrated Circuit Engineering Corporation, "Cost Effective IC Manufacturing 1998–1999," Smithsonian Chip Collection, 1997, 7-4, *http://smithsonianchips.si.edu/ice/cd/CEICM/TITLE.pdf*.

162 Personal notes from SEMI Industry Strategic Symposium Blue Chip Panel, Half Moon Bay, CA, January 12, 2010.

163 Bob Bruck, "Economics and Collaboration Panel," presentation at SEMI Industry Strategic Symposium, Half Moon Bay, CA, January 2010.

164 World Semiconductor Trade Statistics, *http://www.wsts.org*.

165 Graphic based on data from World Semiconductor Trade Statistics, "WSTS Semiconductor Market Forecast Autumn 2009," November 17, 2009, *http://www.wsts.org/PRESS/PRESS-ARCHIVE/WSTS-Semiconductor-Market-Forecast-Autumn-2009* (adapted and data used with permission).

166 IC Insights, "Glossary of Terms," 2002–2008, *http://www.icinsights.com/search/?q=Glossary+of+Terms+2002-2008*; Jerzy Ruzyllo, "Semiconductor Glossary," 2001–2009, *http://www.semi1source.com/glossary/default.asp?whichpage=default*.

167 Semico Research, "Is consolidation the new game for the IC industry?," *EE Times India*, April 7, 2010, *http://www.eetindia.co.in/ART_8800603040_1800007_NT_b69fec09.HTM* (reprinted with permission).

168 Gartner, Inc., "Top 10 Semiconductor Vendors by Revenue Estimates, 2009," in Peter Clarke, "Winners, Losers in 2009 Chip Vendor Ranking," EE Times Asia, March 31, 2010, *http://www.eetasia.com/ART_8800602399_480200_NT_72aebd89.HTM* (adapted and reprinted with permission).

169 IC Insights, Company Reports, "Top 10 Semiconductor Industry Capital Spenders," in "IC Insights: Top 10 to Spend Aggressively in 2010," Semiconductor International, February 24, 2010 (adapted and reprinted with permission from IC Insights).

170 Clair Brown and Greg Linden, *Chips and Change: How Crisis Reshapes the Semiconductor Industry* (Cambridge, MA: MIT Press, 2009).

171 Michael H. Siam-Heng, "Development of China's Semiconductor Industry: Prospects and Problems," in Elspeth Thomson and Jon Sigurdson, *China's Science and Technology Sector and the Forces of Globalization* (Singapore: World Scientific Publishing, 2008), 219.

172 National Academies, *http://www.nationalacademies.org/*.

173 U.S. Bureau of Industry and Security, *www.bis.doc.gov/*.

174 As a side note, many companies are using file names with random hexadecimal code on YouTube, thereby allowing their video clips to "hide in plain sight." Source: Phil Britton, "Integrating Web 2.0 Tools in Your Intelligence Process," Washington, DC: Strategic and Competitive Intelligence Professionals Conference, 2010. Comment during lecture.

175 UBM Electronics, "Enjoy the Show," image screenshot, *EE Times* Virtual Conference: Medical System Design, May 20, 2010, *http://www.eetimes.com/medical/* (reprinted with permission).

ABOUT THE AUTHOR

Charles (Chuck) Howe serves as Deputy Director to the Assistant Deputy Director of National Intelligence Acquisition organization, which is part of the Acquisition, Technology & Facilities organization within the Office of the Director of National Intelligence. Before joining the Intelligence Community, Mr. Howe served in the United States Air Force for 27 years, retiring with the rank of Colonel. He has a long association with the aerospace industry, and capped off his military career teaching at the Industrial College of the Armed Forces (now Dwight D. Eisenhower School for National Security).

www.ingramcontent.com/pod-product-compliance
Lightning Source LLC
Chambersburg PA
CBHW081946070426
42451CB00017BA/3457